The Liturgy of the Hours

The Liturgy of the Hours

The General Instruction on the Liturgy of the Hours

with a

Commentary

by

A.-M. Roguet, O.P.

Translated by Peter Coughlan and Peter Purdue

THE LITURGICAL PRESS
Collegeville, Minnesota

First published 1971

This book is set in Monotype Times.

ISBN 0-8146-0260-6

Contents

Chapter Three The Various Parts of the Liturgy of the Hours

Chapter Four Various Celebrations in the Course of the Year

Part Two

Commentary on the Renewed Liturgy of the Hours

by A.-M. Roguet, O.P.

Chapter Two Liturgy

Chapter Three Spirituality

Introduction

Three factors that from the earliest days have constantly nourished the Church's inner life are the Mass, the sacraments, and the prayer of the Hours.

Mass on the Lord's day has always been the heart and centre of Catholic worship. It brings us into direct and life-giving contact with the paschal mystery of Christ our Lord. The other sacraments mark our encounter with Christ at particularly significant and important moments of our lives. Together with the Mass, these take Christians into the mystery of our Lord's death and resurrection and sanctify their lives.

The prayer of the Hours sanctifies the course of each day. It is a call to praise and reflection at different parts of the day, reminding us constantly of God's loving presence in his Church. The terms 'Divine Office' and 'Breviary' reflect later developments of this prayer of the Hours. St Benedict described this round of daily praise and prayer as the *opus Dei*, the work of God. He saw the Church on earth as joining the praise offered to God by the blessed in heaven.

The awareness of the Liturgy of the Hours as something belonging essentially to the whole Church, has, regrettably, hardly been in evidence for many centuries. It had come to be considered as the preserve of religious and clergy. Liturgical services however are not private functions, or reserved to groups of élites, they are celebrations of the Church which is the 'sacrament of unity'. They pertain to the whole body of the Church, although they concern different members of the Church in different ways according to the diversity of holy orders, functions, and degrees of participation.

As can be seen from the very structure of the Hours, with their psalms, readings, hymns, responsories and prayers, they are designed for celebration in common. Individual recitation came in only when this communal celebration was not possible.

The liturgical reform seeks to restore the Liturgy of the Hours as a celebration of the whole Church community, the holy people of God. This is the purpose of the renewed Liturgy of the Hours which is offered to the whole Church in 1971.

The present volume contains both a translation of the new *General Instruction on the Liturgy of the Hours*, and a Commentary upon this new reform.

The Commentary was prepared by Father A.-M. Roguet, O.P., who from the time of the preparatory commission up to the present has actively collaborated in the liturgical reform. Fr Roguet is not only an excellent theologian and liturgist, he is also a brilliant popularizer, since he knows how to present even the most abstract theological ideas in an attractive and digestible way. The present Commentary is yet another example of his work. In preparing it, he has been able to take into account the documentation prepared by the nine study-groups which have brought the *opus ingens et fascinosum* to its conclusion, and to have the advice of those *ignoti milites*, who have generously worked on this project.

I should like to thank Peter Coughlan and Peter Purdue for having accepted the request that they undertake this translation, and for having done the work with speed and efficiency. In various capacities they have been closely connected with the liturgical reform since 1965, first with the Post-conciliar Liturgy Consilium, and more recently with the Congregation for Divine Worship. They are already known for their writings and recordings on the Mass, the Eucharistic Prayers, and the Lectionary.

I commend both General Instruction and Commentary to the reflection of many readers. They constitute a very useful introduction to the reform of the Liturgy of the Hours. May all who read them come to a more lively appreciation of this renewed prayer of the Hours, and so come closer to Christ, the Alpha and the Omega.

A. Bugnini

Secretary of the Sacred Congregation for Divine Worship

Translators' Note

When the phrase 'Liturgy of the Hours' is used in this translation of the General Instruction, it refers both to the divine Office and to the volumes which will contain this Office. When the phrase is italicized, it refers to the volumes containing the Office; when not italicized, the phrase applies to the Office itself. In the General Instruction the Latin text often has *Laudes matutinae* as well as *Laudes*; in this translation we have simply used Lauds for both.

The present translation of the General Instruction was prepared at the request of the Sacred Congregation for Divine Worship. It may be of use until an official translation has been prepared by the competent translation committees of the English-speaking hierarchies.

We should like to express our sincere gratitude for the assistance of Laurence Brandt and Frances Kenny in helping to prepare this translation.

Part One

The General Instruction on The Liturgy of the Hours

SACRED CONGREGATION FOR DIVINE WORSHIP
Prot. 165/71

Since a further period of time is still required before the publication of the volumes of the Divine Office or *The Liturgy of the Hours* is possible, on account of the magnitude of the work involved and difficulties connected with it, this Sacred Congregation, by special mandate of his Holiness Pope Paul VI, has decided to anticipate in a separate volume the *General Instruction on the Liturgy of the Hours*, which will subsequently have its place at the beginning of the first volume.

Thus priests, religious and the faithful, whether individually or in groups gathered for study or prayer, may have the opportunity to familiarize themselves with the values of this new book of the Church, its special structure and the norms for celebrating the Liturgy of the Hours, as well as the spiritual benefits the people of God will gain from it.

From the Offices of the Sacred Congregation of Divine Worship, 2 *February* 1971, *the Presentation of our Lord.*

A. BUGNINI
Secretary

Chapter One

The Importance of the Liturgy of the Hours or the Divine Office in the Life of the Church

1. The public and communal prayer of the people of God is rightly considered among the first duties of the Church. From the very beginning the baptized 'remained faithful to the teaching of the apostles, to the brotherhood, to the breaking of bread and to the prayers' (Acts 2:42). Many times the Acts of the Apostles testifies that the Christian community prayed together.[1]

The testimony of the early Church shows that individual faithful also devoted themselves to prayer at certain hours. In various areas the practice soon gained ground of devoting special times to prayer in common. These were, for example, at the last hour of the day at dusk when the lamps were lighted, or at the first hour of the day when the rising sun dispelled the last shadow of night.

In the course of time other hours were also sanctified by communal prayer, hours which the Fathers judged were found in the Acts of the Apostles. For in the Acts the disciples are presented as coming together at the third hour.[2] The prince of apostles 'went to the housetop at about the sixth hour to pray' (10:9); 'Peter and John were going up to the Temple for the prayers at the ninth hour' (3:1); 'late that night Paul and Silas were praying and singing God's praises' (16:25).

2. These prayers in common gradually took on a more definite shape, which today we describe as 'the course of the Hours'. This Liturgy of the Hours, or Divine Office, further enriched with readings, is principally a prayer of praise and supplication, indeed it is the prayer of the Church with Christ and to Christ.

I. The Prayer of Christ

The prayer of Christ to the Father

3. Since he came to give the life of God to men, the Word who is the radiant light proceeding from the Father's glory, 'Christ

[1] Footnotes will be found on pp. 70ff.

Jesus, high priest of the new and eternal covenant, taking human nature, introduced into this earthly exile that hymn which is sung throughout all ages in the halls of heaven'.[3] Thus in the heart of Christ the praise of God finds expression in human words of adoration, propitiation and intercession; the head of renewed humanity and mediator of God prays to the Father in the name and for the good of all mankind.

4. The Son of God himself 'who is one with his Father' (cf. John 10:30), who entering the world said, 'Here I am! I am coming, O God, to obey your will' (Hebrews 10:9; cf. John 6:38), deigned to show us how he prayed. Again and again the Gospels tell us that he prayed: when his mission from the Father is revealed;[4] before he calls the apostles;[5] when he blesses God at the multiplication of the loaves;[6] when he is transfigured on the mountain;[7] when he heals the deaf-mute;[8] when he raises Lazarus from the dead;[9] before he asks Peter's confession of faith;[10] when he teaches his disciples to pray;[11] when the disciples return from their mission;[12] when he blesses little children;[13] and when he prays for Peter.[14]

His daily activity was closely bound up with prayer, and may be said to have flowed from it; we see this when he went into the desert or the hills to pray;[15] we are also told that he rose early in the morning to pray,[16] and that he even spent the night in prayer to God,[17] remaining until the fourth watch.[18]

He too, as we well know, took part in the public prayers of the synagogue – when 'as was his custom'[19] he entered on the sabbath – and in the prayers of the temple which he called a house of prayer.[20] He also said those private prayers which pious Jews were accustomed to say every day. He said the customary blessings over meals, as is expressly narrated in the multiplication of the loaves,[21] at the Last Supper,[22] and at the meal in Emmaus;[23] he likewise sang the psalms with his disciples.[24]

Even at the very end of his life, as his Passion was approaching,[25] at the Last Supper,[26] during his agony in the garden,[27] and on the cross,[28] the divine Master showed that prayer was what animated his messianic ministry and paschal sacrifice. 'During his life on earth, he offered up prayer and entreaty, aloud and in silent tears, to the one who had the power to save him out of death, and he submitted so humbly that his prayer was heard' (Hebrews 5:7), and by virtue of his perfect offering on the altar of the cross, 'he has achieved the eternal perfection of all whom he is sanctifying' (Hebrews 10:14). Now raised from the dead, he is living forever to intercede for us all.[29]

II. The Prayer of the Church

The obligation to pray

5. What Jesus himself did, he also commands us to do. He often said, 'Pray', 'Ask', 'Seek',[30] 'in my name'.[31] He gave us the Lord's Prayer to teach us how to pray.[32] He instructed us on the necessity of prayer,[33] and told us to be humble,[34] watchful,[35] persevering and confident in the goodness of the Father,[36] pure in intention and worthy of God.[37]

Throughout their Letters, the apostles give us many prayers, especially of praise and thanksgiving. They enjoin us to offer prayer to God the Father,[38] through Christ,[39] in the Holy Spirit,[40] with constancy and perseverance,[41] pointing out its efficacy for our sanctification.[42] They admonish us to praise[43] and thank God[44], and to offer petitions[45] and intercessions for everyone.[46]

The Church continues the prayer of Christ

6. Since man is totally dependent upon God, he must acknowledge and confess the dominion of his creator over him. This is what holy men have done in every age through prayer.

Prayer directed to God should be united with Christ, the Lord of all men, the one mediator,[47] through whom alone we have access to God.[48] Christ so unites the whole human family to himself[49] that there is an intimate and necessary relationship between the prayer of Christ and the prayer of the whole human race. For in Christ alone human religion achieves its redemptive value and purpose.

7. A close and special bond exists between Christ and those whom, through the sacrament of regeneration, he makes members of his body, the Church. All the riches belonging to the Son flow from him as from the head into the whole body: the pouring out of the Spirit, truth, life and a share in his divine sonship, which he revealed to us in all his prayer on earth.

The whole body of the Church shares in the priesthood of Christ. The baptized, by regeneration and the anointing of the

Holy Spirit, are consecrated into a spiritual house and a holy priesthood.[50] They become capable of taking part in the worship of the New Testament, not thanks to themselves, but to the gift and merits of Christ.

'God could give men no greater gift than to make his Word, through whom he created all things, their head, that they in turn should become his members. The Son of God has become the Son of Man, one God with the Father, one man with men; so that when we speak to God in prayer, the Son is not separated from the Father; when the Body of the Son prays, the head is not separated from the body. It is the one saviour of his body, our Lord Jesus Christ, who prays for us, prays in us, and is prayed to by us. He prays for us as our priest. He prays in us as our head. He is prayed to by us as our God. Let us recognize therefore our voices in him and his voice in us.'[51]

Christian prayer draws its dignity from its sharing in the filial relationship of the Only-Begotten Son to the Father. The prayer he expressed in his earthly life with his own words in the name of and for the salvation of the entire human race, he continues to address to his Father in the whole Church and in all her members.

The action of the Holy Spirit

8. The unity of the praying Church is brought about by the Holy Spirit, the same Spirit who is in Christ,[52] in the whole Church, and in each baptized person. 'This Spirit comes to help us in our weakness' and 'expresses our plea in a way that could never be put into words' (Romans 8:26). As the Spirit of the Son, he breathes into us 'the spirit of adopted sons, and makes us cry out, "Abba, Father!" ' (Romans 8:15; cf. Galatians 4:6; I Corinthians 12:3; Ephesians 5:18; Jude 20). There can be no Christian prayer without the action of the Holy Spirit. He unites the whole Church and leads us through the Son to the Father.

The community character of prayer

9. The example and command of the Lord and his apostles to persevere in continuous prayer are not to be considered a mere legal rule. Prayer expresses the very essence of the Church as a community. When the community of the faithful is first mentioned in the Acts of the Apostles, it is described as gathered together in prayer 'with several women, including Mary the Mother of Jesus, and with his brothers' (Acts 1:14). 'The whole group of believers was united, heart and soul' (Acts 4:32). Their common brotherhood was based upon the word of God, prayer and the Eucharist.[53]

The private prayer[54] of the members of the Church is offered to the Father through Christ in the Holy Spirit, and as such is always necessary and to be commended.[55] Community prayer, however, has a special dignity since Christ himself said: 'Where two or three meet in my name, I shall be there with them' (Mt 18:20).

III. The Liturgy of the Hours

The consecration of time

10. Christ told us 'about the need to pray continually and never lose heart' (Luke 18:1). The Church has faithfully heeded this exhortation by never ceasing in her prayer and by urging us to pray: 'Through him (Jesus), let us offer God an unending sacrifice of praise' (Hebrews 13:15). The Church not only satisfies this precept by celebrating the Eucharist, but also in other different ways, especially the Liturgy of the Hours. Compared with other liturgical actions, the particular characteristic which ancient tradition has attached to the Liturgy of the Hours is that it should consecrate the course of day and night.[56]

11. Because the purpose of the Office is to sanctify the day and all human activity, the traditional sequence of the Hours has been so restored that, as far as possible, they may be genuinely related to the time of the day at which they are prayed. The modern conditions in which daily life has to be lived has also been taken into account.[57]

Consequently, 'that the day may be truly sanctified, and that the Hours themselves may be recited with spiritual advantage, it is best that each of them be prayed at a time which most clearly corresponds with its true canonical time'.[58]

The relationship between the Eucharist and the Liturgy of the Hours

12. The Liturgy of the Hours extends[59] to the different hours of the day the praise and prayer, the memorial of the mysteries of salvation and the foretaste of heavenly glory, which are offered us in the eucharistic mystery, 'the centre and culmination of the whole life of the Christian community'.[60]

The Liturgy of the Hours is in itself an excellent preparation for the celebration of the Eucharist. It fosters those dispositions necessary for a fruitful participation in the Eucharist, such as faith, hope and love, devotion and a spirit of sacrifice.

The exercise of Christ's priestly office in the Liturgy of the Hours

13. Christ accomplishes 'the work of redeeming mankind and giving perfect glory to God'[61] in the Holy Spirit through the Church not only when the Eucharist is celebrated and the sacraments administered, but also in other ways, especially by praying the Liturgy of the Hours.[62] Christ is present when his community comes together, when the word of God is proclaimed and 'when the Church prays and sings'.[63]

The sanctification of man

14. The sanctification of man and the worship of God is achieved[64] in the Liturgy of the Hours by the setting up of a dialogue between God and man, so that 'God speaks to his people . . . and the people reply to God both by song and by prayer'.[65]

The saving word of God has great importance in the Liturgy of the Hours, and may be of enormous spiritual benefit for those taking part. From sacred scripture the readings are chosen; the words of God in the psalms are sung in his presence; the prayers, collects and liturgical chants draw their inspiration from the same source.[66]

'Not only when things are read "which have been written for our instruction' (Romans 15:4), but also when the Church prays or sings or acts, the faith of those taking part is nourished and their minds are raised to God, so that they may offer him the worship which reason requires and more copiously receive his grace.'[67]

The praise given to God, in union with the Church in heaven

15. In the Liturgy of the Hours, the Church exercises the priestly office of her head and constantly[68] offers God a sacrifice of praise, 'a verbal sacrifice that is offered every time we acknowledge his name'.[69] This prayer is 'the voice of the bride addressing her bridegroom; it is the very prayer which Christ himself, together with his body, addresses to the Father.'[70] 'Hence all who perform this service are not only fulfilling the duty of the Church, but also are sharing in the greatest honour accorded to Christ's spouse, for by offering these praises to God they are standing before God's throne in the name of the Church their Mother.'[71]

16. By offering praise to God in the Hours, the Church joins in singing that canticle of praise which is sung throughout all ages in the halls of heaven;[72] it is a foretaste of the heavenly praise sung unceasingly before the throne of God and the Lamb, as described by John in the Apocalypse. Our intimate union with the Church in heaven is put into effect when 'with common rejoicing we celebrate together the praise of the divine Majesty; then all those from every tribe and tongue and people and nation (cf. Apocalypse 5:9) who have been redeemed by the blood of Christ and gathered together into one Church, with one song of praise magnify the one and triune God'.[73]

This heavenly liturgy was seen by the prophets as a victory of day over night, of light over darkness: 'no more will the sun give you daylight, nor moonlight shine on you, but the Lord will be your everlasting light, your God will be your splendour' (Isaiah 60:19; cf. Apocalypse 21:23,25). 'It will be a day of wonder – the Lord knows it – with no alternation of day and night; in the evening it will be light' (Zechariah 14:7). 'The final age of the world has already come upon us (cf. I Corinthians 10:11). The renovation of the world has been irrevocably decreed and in this age is already anticipated in some real way.'[74] Therefore our faith teaches us the meaning of our earthly existence, so that we may await with every creature the revelation of the sons of God.[75] In the Liturgy of the Hours we proclaim this faith, we express and nurture this hope, and we share the joy of giving unceasing praise in the day which knows no end.

Supplication and Intercession

17. As well as praising God, the Church's liturgy expresses the hopes and prayers of all the Christian faithful and intercedes before Christ and through him before the Father for the salvation of the whole world.[76] This voice is not only of the Church but of Christ. It is in the name of Christ that she prays, that is, 'through Jesus Christ our Lord,' and so the Church continues to offer that prayer and entreaty which Christ offered during his life on earth,[77] and which therefore has a unique effectiveness. Thus the Church community exercises a true motherhood towards souls who are to be led to Christ, not only by charity, example and works of penance, but also by prayer.[78]

These things pertain above all to those who by special mandate are deputed to celebrate the Liturgy of the Hours, namely: bishops and priests, who by reason of their office pray for those entrusted to them and for the whole people of God,[79] other sacred ministers, and religious.[80]

The culmination and source of pastoral activity

18. Whoever participates in the Liturgy of the Hours makes the Lord's people grow by imparting to them a hidden apostolic fruitfulness.[81] 'For the goal of apostolic works is that all who are made sons of God by faith and baptism should come together to praise God in the midst of his Church, to take part in her sacrifice, and to eat the Lord's supper.'[82] The faithful thus express in their lives and manifest to others 'the mystery of Christ and the real nature of the true Church. It is of the essence of the Church that she be both . . . visible and yet invisibly endowed, eager to act and yet devoted to contemplation, present in this world and yet not at home in it.'[83]

The readings and prayers of the Liturgy of the Hours constitute in turn a wellspring of the Christian life. From the table of sacred scripture and the words of the saints this life is nourished, and by prayer it is strengthened. The Lord alone, without whom we can do nothing,[84] can if we ask him give fruitfulness and increase to the works in which we are engaged.[85] Day by day we are built into the Temple of God in the Spirit[86] until Christ's full stature is achieved[87] and we are strengthened to preach Christ to those who are outside.[88]

Heart and voice are one

19. Those taking part in this prayer should make it their own so that it becomes a source of devotion, abundant grace and nourishment for personal prayer and apostolic activity. In praying it worthily, attentively and with devotion, they must attune their minds to their voices.[89] If the grace of God is not to be fruitless in them, they must wholeheartedly cooperate with it. They must seek God and penetrate ever more deeply through prayer into the mystery of Christ.[90] With that same mind which was in our Redeemer, they should praise God and pray to him.

IV. Those Who Celebrate the Liturgy of the Hours

a. Celebration in Common

20. The Liturgy of the Hours, like the other liturgical services, is not a private function, but pertains to the whole body of the Church. It manifests the Church and has an effect upon it.[91] Its ecclesial celebration is best seen and especially recommended when it is performed – with the bishop surrounded by his priests and ministers[92] – by the local Church, 'in which the one, holy, catholic and apostolic Church of Christ is truly present and operative.'[93] Even when the bishop is absent and it is celebrated by the chapter of canons or by other priests, the genuine relationship of the Hours to the time of day should be maintained and as far as possible it should be with the participation of the people. The same should be said of collegiate chapters.

21. Among other groups of the faithful, parishes – which could be called cells of the diocese – set up locally under a pastor who takes the place of the bishop are most important, and 'in a certain way they represent the visible Church as it is established throughout the world'.[94] Wherever possible the more important hours could be celebrated in common at the church.

22. If the faithful come together and unite their hearts and voices in the Liturgy of the Hours, they manifest the Church celebrating the mystery of Christ.[95]

23. The task of those who are in sacred orders or who have a special canonical mission[96] is to direct and preside over the prayer of the community; 'they should devote their labour to this end, that all those committed to their care may be of one mind in prayer'.[97] Pastors of souls should see to it that the faithful are invited and helped by requisite instruction to celebrate the chief Hours in common, especially on Sundays and feasts.[98] They should teach them to draw sincere prayer from their participation[99] and so help them to understand the psalms in a Christian way that they may gradually come to use and appreciate the prayer of the Church more fully.[100]

24. Communities of canons, monks, nuns and other religious, who by virtue of their rule or constitution celebrate the Liturgy of the Hours either wholly or in part according to the common or a special rite, represent the Church at prayer in a special way. As the exemplar of the Church which unceasingly praises God with one voice, they more fully show and fulfil the duty of working, especially by prayer, for 'the building up and increasing of the whole mystical Body of Christ and the good of the particular Churches.'[101] This is especially true of those engaged in the contemplative life.

25. Sacred ministers and all clerics, not otherwise bound to common celebration, who live together or assemble for any purpose, should try to say at least some part of the Liturgy of the Hours in common, particularly Lauds in the morning and Vespers in the evening.[102]

26. Even religious of both sexes, who are not obliged to celebration in common, and members of any Institution dedicated to acquiring perfection are strongly recommended to gather together by themselves or with the people to celebrate this Liturgy or part of it.

27. Wherever groups of the laity are gathered and whatever the reason which has brought them together, such as prayer or the apostolate, they are encouraged to recite the Church's Office, by celebrating part of the Liturgy of the Hours.[103] For they should learn to adore God the Father in spirit and in truth[104] especially through liturgical worship; they must remember that by public worship and prayer they can have an impact on all men and contribute to the salvation of the whole world.[105]

Finally, it is fitting that the family, as the domestic sanctuary of the Church, should not only offer common prayer to God but also say certain parts of the Liturgy of the Hours, in this way uniting themselves more closely to the Church.[106]

b. The Mandate of Celebrating the Liturgy of the Hours

28. The Liturgy of the Hours is entrusted to sacred ministers in a special way so that it is to be recited by each of them – with the necessary adaptations – even when the people are not present. The Church deputes them to say the Liturgy of the Hours in order that at least through them the duty of the whole community may be constantly and continuously fulfilled and the prayer of Christ may persevere unceasingly in the Church.[107]

The bishop represents the person of Christ in an eminent and visible way and is the high priest of his flock. In a certain sense it is from him that the faithful who are under his care derive and maintain their life in Christ.[108] Therefore the bishop should be the first in prayer among the members of his Church. When he recites the Liturgy of the Hours he always does so in the name of and on behalf of the Church committed to him.[109]

Priests, united to the bishop and the whole presbyterium, also represent the person of Christ the priest in a special way.[110] They share the same duty of praying to God on behalf of all the people entrusted to them and indeed for the whole world.[111]

All these fulfil the ministry of the Good Shepherd, who asks for his own that they may have life and that they may be completely one.[112] In the Liturgy of the Hours, presented to them by the Church, they not only find a source of devotion and nourishment for personal prayer,[113] but also a wealth of contemplation to feed and foster their pastoral and missionary activities, to the joy of the whole Church of God.[114]

29. Bishops and priests, therefore, and the other sacred ministers, who have received from the Church the mandate to celebrate the Liturgy of the Hours (cf. n. 17), are to recite the whole sequence of Hours each day, preserving as far as possible the genuine relationship of the Hours to the time of day.

They are to give due importance to the Hours which are the two hinges on which this Liturgy turns, that is, Lauds as morning prayer and Vespers; let them take care not to omit these Hours, unless for a serious reason.

They are also to carry out faithfully the Office of Readings, which is above all the liturgical celebration of the word of God Thus they will carry out daily that duty of welcoming into themselves the word of God. This makes them more perfect disciples of the Lord and wins them a deeper knowledge of the unfathomable riches of Christ.[115]

That the day may be completely sanctified, they will desire to recite the middle Hour and Compline, thus commending themselves to God and completing the entire 'Opus Dei' before going to bed.

30. It is most fitting that permanent deacons should recite some part of the Liturgy of the Hours each day as determined by the Episcopal Conference.[116]

31. a) Cathedral and collegiate chapters are bound to recite those parts of the Liturgy of the Hours in choir which are imposed upon them by general or particular law.

Besides the Hours which are to be recited by all sacred ministers, each member of these chapters is obliged to recite individually those hours to which his chapter is bound.[117]

b) Religious communities, and their single members, bound to recite the Liturgy of the Hours, are to celebrate the Hours in accordance with their particular law. Regarding those in sacred orders the norms of n. 29 also obtain.

32. Other religious communities and their individual members are to be encouraged, according to the circumstances in which they find themselves, to celebrate some part of the Liturgy of the Hours which is the prayer of the Church, so that Christians everywhere are united heart and soul.[118]

The same encouragement is to be given to the laity.[119]

c. The Structure of the Celebration

33. The Liturgy of the Hours is structured according to its own laws. In a special way it combines those elements which are in other Christian celebrations. It is arranged as follows: the opening hymn; psalmody; a shorter or longer reading of sacred scriptures; prayers.

Whether it is celebrated in common or in private, the essential structure of this Liturgy is a dialogue between God and man. Celebration in common shows more clearly the ecclesial nature of the Liturgy of the Hours. It fosters the active participation of all according to their individual circumstances through acclamations, dialogues, alternating psalmody and other things of this kind, and takes into account various forms of expression.[120] As often as the communal celebration may take place with the presence and active participation of the faithful, it is to be preferred to individual and quasi-private celebration.[121] It is fitting  that the Office both in choir and in common be sung, when this is possible, in accordance with the nature of each of its parts and the function of each participant.

In this way the wish of the apostle is fulfilled: ‘Let the message of Christ, in all its richness, find a home with you. Teach each other, and advise each other, in all wisdom. With gratitude in your hearts sing psalms and hymns and inspired songs to God’ (Colossians 3:16; cf. Ephesians 5:19–20).

Chapter Two

The Sanctification of the Day – The Various Liturgical Hours

I. The Introduction to the Whole Office

34. The whole Office is normally begun with an invitatory. This consists in the verse *Domine, labia mea aperies: Et os meum annuntiabit laudem tuam*, and Ps 94. This invitatory verse and psalm daily invite the faithful to sing the praises of God, hear his voice and look forward to the 'Rest of the Lord'.[1]

If desired, Ps 99, Ps 66 or Ps 23 may be used in place of Ps 94.

As indicated elsewhere, it is fitting that the invitatory psalm be said in responsorial fashion, that is, with its antiphon said first, repeated, and taken up again after each verse of the psalm.

35. The invitatory should begin the whole sequence of daily prayer; thus it begins Lauds or the Office of Readings depending on which of these liturgical actions begins the day. If so desired, however, the psalm with its antiphon may be omitted when it comes before Lauds.

36. The way of varying the invitatory antiphon, according to the different liturgical days, is indicated in its proper place.

II. Lauds and Vespers

37. 'By the venerable tradition of the universal Church, Lauds as morning prayer and Vespers as evening prayer are the two hinges on which the daily Office turns; hence they are to be considered as the chief Hours and are to be celebrated as such.'[2]

38. Lauds is designed and structured to sanctify the morning, as is clear from many of its parts. St Basil the Great excellently described its character as morning prayer in these words: 'Matins consecrates to God the first movements of our minds and hearts; no other care should engage us before we have been moved with the thought of God, as it is written, "I thought of God and sighed" (Ps 76:4), nor should the body undertake any work before we have done what is said, "I say this prayer to you, Lord, for at daybreak you listen for my voice; and at dawn I hold myself in readiness for you, I watch for you" (Ps 5:4–5).'[3]

This Hour, recited as the light of a new day dawns, recalls the resurrection of the Lord Jesus, the true light, enlightening every man (cf. John 1:9), 'the Sun of Justice' (Malachy 4:2), 'arising on high' (Luke 1:78). Thus the remark of St Cyprian may be well understood: 'We should pray in the morning to celebrate the resurrection of the Lord with morning prayer.'[4]

39. Vespers is celebrated in the evening when the day is drawing to a close, so that 'we may give thanks for what has been given us during the day, or for the things we have done well during it'.[5] We also call to mind our redemption, through the prayer we offer 'like incense in the sight of the Lord', and in which 'the raising up of our hands' becomes 'an evening sacrifice'. This 'evening sacrifice' 'may be more fully understood as that true evening sacrifice which was given in the evening by our Lord and Saviour when he instituted the most holy mysteries of the Church at supper with his apostles; or which on the following day he offered for all time to his Father by the raising up of his hands for the salvation of the whole world.'[7] Placing our hope in that Sun which never sets, 'we pray and beg that his light may shine on us again; we pray that Christ may come bringing the grace of eternal light'.[8] Finally, in this Hour, we join with the Eastern Churches and invoke 'blessed Jesus Christ, the Light of our Heavenly Father's sacred and eternal glory; as the sun sets we behold the evening light and sing to God, Father, Son and Holy Spirit . . .'.

40. In the prayer of the Christian community, Lauds and Vespers are of the highest importance. Their public and common celebration should be encouraged especially among those who lead a common life. The recitation of these prayers is also recommended for the individual faithful who are not able to participate in a common celebration.

41. Lauds and Vespers begin with the introductory verse *Deus, in adiutorium meum intende: Domine, ad adiuvandum me festina.* The *Gloria Patri* and *Sicut erat* with *Alleluia* follow. The *Alleluia* is omitted during Lent. This form of introduction is not used when the Invitatory immediately precedes Lauds.

42. A suitable hymn is then said. The hymn should be composed so as to express the particular characteristic of each Hour or feast. It makes an easy and pleasant opening to the prayer, especially in celebrations with the people.

43. The psalmody follows the hymn, in accordance with the norms of nn. 121–125. The psalmody of Lauds consists of one morning psalm, followed by an Old Testament canticle, and a second psalm which traditionally is one of praise.

The psalmody of Vespers consists of two psalms or two sections of longer psalms, well suited to the Hour and to celebration with the people, followed by a canticle from the Epistles or the Apocalypse.

44. There is a short or long reading after the psalmody.

45. A short reading is given according to the liturgical day, season or feast. It is to be read and heard as the true proclamation of the word of God; it emphasizes certain passages and helps to highlight short sayings which receive less attention in the continuous reading of the scriptures.

The short readings vary according to the daily arrangement of the psalmody.

46. A longer scripture reading may be chosen, especially for celebrations with the people. It may be taken from the Office of Readings or from the passage read at Mass, and especially from those texts left unread for various reasons. On occasion, there is no reason why a more suitable reading may not be chosen in accordance with the norms of nn. 248–249, 251.

47. In celebrations with the people, a brief homily may be added to explain the reading.

48. After the reading or homily, there may be a silent pause.

49. In response to the word of God, there may be a responsorial song, or short responsory. This may be omitted if so desired.

Other songs of the same type and for the same purpose may replace the responsory, provided that these are duly approved by the Episcopal Conference.

50. A Gospel canticle is then solemnly recited with its antiphon; at Lauds it is the Canticle of Zechariah, the *Benedictus*; at Vespers the Canticle of the Blessed Virgin Mary, the *Magnificat*. These canticles express praise and thanksgiving for our redemption and have been in popular use for centuries in the Roman Church. The antiphons for the *Benedictus* and the *Magnificat* vary according to the liturgical day, season or feast.

51. After the canticle: at Lauds, Prayers consecrate the day and its work to God; at Vespers there are Prayers of intercession (cf. nn. 179–193).

52. After the Prayers or Intercessions, the *Pater Noster* is said by all.

53. A concluding prayer immediately follows the *Pater Noster*; for ordinary ferial days it is found in the Psalter; for other days in the Proper.

54. If a priest or deacon is present, he dismisses the people as at Mass with the greeting *Dominus vobiscum* and a Blessing; there follows the invitation *Ite in pace. R. Deo gratias.* Otherwise the celebration is concluded with *Dominus nos benedicat*, etc.

III. The Office of Readings

55. The purpose of the Office of Readings is to present to the people of God, and particularly to those who are consecrated to God in a special way, a more extensive meditation on sacred scripture and on the best writings of spiritual authors. Even though a more ample series of scripture readings is read daily at Mass, the treasures of revelation and tradition contained in the Office of Readings greatly assist spiritual progress. Priests especially should explore these riches. They will then be able to teach everyone the word of God they themselves have received and make their doctrine 'the food of the people of God'.[9]

56. Prayer should accompany the reading of sacred scripture to make it a conversation between God and man; 'we speak to him when we pray, we hear him when we read the divine words'.[10] Thus the Office of Readings consists in psalms, a hymn, a collect and other formulas, and has the character of true prayer.

57. According to the Constitution *Sacrosanctum Concilium*, the Office of Readings, 'although it should retain the character of nocturnal praise when celebrated in choir, should be adapted so that it may be recited at any hour of the day; it is to be made up of fewer psalms and longer readings'.[11]

58. Those who by reason of their particular law must preserve the character of nocturnal praise in the Office of Readings, and who praiseworthily wish to do so – whether they say it at night or very early in the morning before Lauds – should select a hymn from time 'throughout the year' from the series indicated for this purpose. For Sundays, solemnities and certain feasts, nn. 70–73 concerning vigils should be taken into account.

59. Excepting the cases just mentioned, the Office of Readings may be recited at any hour of the day, or even in the night hours of the preceding day, after Vespers.

60. If the Office of Readings is said before Lauds, it is preceded by the invitatory as indicated above (nn. 34–36). Otherwise it begins with the verse *Deus, in adiutorium* with the *Gloria, Sicut erat*, and (outside of Lent) the *Alleluia.*

61. A hymn is then said. In time 'throughout the year' it is chosen either from the series for recitation at night, as indicated above in n. 58, or from the day series, thus respecting the correct time.

62. The Psalmody follows, consisting of three psalms (or sections of longer psalms). In the Paschal Triduum, on octave days of Easter and Christmas, and on solemnities and feasts, the psalms are proper and have proper antiphons.

On Sundays and ferial days, the psalms and antiphons are taken from the current Psalter. The psalms and antiphons are also taken from the current psalter on the memorials of saints, unless these are proper (cf. nn. 218ff).

63. A versicle is normally said between the psalmody and the readings. In this way the prayer is provided with a transition from the psalmody to listening to the readings.

64. There are two readings: the first is from the scriptures, the second is either from the works of the Fathers or Church writers, or is hagiographical.

65. A responsory is said after each reading (cf. nn. 169–172).

66. The scripture reading is normally taken from the Proper of the Season, following the norms below, nn. 140–155. On solemnities and feasts, this reading is taken from the Proper or from the Common.

67. The second reading with its responsory is taken either from *The Liturgy of the Hours*, or from the optional Lectionary dealt with in n. 161 below. Normally it is from the Proper of the Season.

On solemnities and feasts, a proper hagiographical reading is used; if this is lacking, the second reading is taken from the respective Common of Saints. On memorials of saints, whose celebration is not impeded, a hagiographical reading is again chosen in place of the current second reading (cf. nn. 166, 235).

68. On Sundays outside of Lent, octave days of Easter and Christmas, solemnities and feasts, the *Te Deum* is said after the second reading with its responsory. This hymn is omitted on memorials and ferial days. The final part of the hymn, i.e. from the verse *Salvum fac populum tuum*, may be omitted if desired.

69. The Office of Readings is concluded with the proper prayer of the day, and, at least in common recitation, with the acclamation *Benedicamus Domino. R. Deo gratias.*

IV. Vigils

70. The Paschal Vigil is celebrated by the whole Church, as described in the respective liturgical books. 'The vigil of this night is so important,' says St Augustine, 'that it is called The Vigil as if demanding exclusively for itself a term which is common to the rest.'[12] 'We spend that night in vigil, the night on which the Lord rose, and began for us in his own flesh that life where there is neither death nor sleep. Therefore, as we sing in our long vigil to him who has risen, so we will reign with him in life without end.'[13]

71. From the Paschal Vigil the custom grew in different Churches of beginning certain solemnities with a vigil, especially Christmas and Pentecost. This custom is to be preserved and encouraged according to the special traditions of each Church. Wherever it is fitting to celebrate vigils for other solemnities and pilgrimages, the general norms for the celebration of the word of God should be observed.

72. The Fathers and spiritual writers have very often exhorted the faithful, especially those who lead a contemplative life, to pray at night. By this they seek to encourage them to look forward to the Lord's coming: 'At midnight there was a cry, "The bridegroom is here! go out to meet him" (Matthew 25:6).' 'So stay awake, because you do not know when the master of the house is coming, evening, midnight, cockcrow, dawn; if he comes unexpectedly, he must not find you asleep' (Mark 13:35–36). It is therefore praiseworthy to retain the nocturnal character of the Office of Readings.

73. In the Roman Rite, out of consideration especially for those engaged in apostolic work, the Office of Readings is always of the same length. Those who wish to adhere to the tradition of marking the vigil of a Sunday, solemnity or feast with a more extended celebration should proceed in the following way.

Firstly, the Office of Readings should be celebrated as in *The Liturgy of the Hours* as far as the readings inclusively. After both readings and before the *Te Deum*, canticles may be added, selected from the appropriate appendix of *The Liturgy of the Hours*. A Gospel passage is then read, followed, if desired, by a homily; afterwards the *Te Deum* is sung and the prayer said.

The Gospel on solemnities and feasts is taken from the Lectionary of the Mass; on Sundays it is taken from the series on the paschal mystery found in the Appendix of the book.

V. Terce, Sext and None, or the Middle Hour

74. In imitation of the Apostolic Church and from the earliest times, Christians in their private devotions have, even in the midst of their work, dedicated various moments to prayer throughout the course of the day. This tradition has been associated in different ways with liturgical celebrations.

75. Liturgical custom in both East and West has especially retained Terce, Sext and None, principally because these hours commemorated the events of our Lord's Passion and the first preaching of the Gospel.

76. The Second Vatican Council laid down that the little Hours of Terce, Sext and None should be preserved in choir.[14]

The liturgical practice of saying these three Hours is retained by those who lead a contemplative life, unless particular law indicates otherwise. This is also recommended for everyone, especially for those who take part in retreats and pastoral gatherings.

77. Outside of choir, however, one of the three Hours corresponding to the time of day may be chosen, unless particular law indicates otherwise.

At least one of the Hours is to be celebrated by those who do not say all three, so as to preserve the tradition of praying in the middle of the day's work.

78. The way of saying Terce, Sext and None is drawn up to meet the needs both of those who say only one Hour as the

Middle Hour, and of those who must or wish to celebrate all three Hours.

79. Terce, Sext and None, or the Middle Hour, begin with the introductory verse *Deus, in adiutorium* with the *Gloria, Sicut erat* and (outside of Lent) the *Alleluia.* Then a hymn is said corresponding to the Hour. After this comes the Psalmody, then a short reading followed by a versicle. The Hour is concluded with a prayer, and at least in common recitation, by the acclamation *Benedicamus Domino. R. Deo gratias.*

80. The various hymns and prayers put forward for each Hour are so drawn up as to correspond to the time of day at which they are traditionally celebrated, and so as to provide effectively for the sanctification of the day. Those who say only one of the Hours should choose those parts which correspond more suitably with the Hour celebrated.

The short readings and prayers vary according to the liturgical day, season or feast.

81. Two psalmodies are given: one current, the other complementary. Those who say only one Hour use the current psalmody; those who say two or three Hours use the current psalmody for one, and the complementary psalmody for the others.

82. The current psalmody consists of three psalms (or parts of longer psalms) from the current Psalter. These psalms have their own antiphons, unless otherwise indicated.

On solemnities, during the Paschal Triduum and on octave days of Easter, proper antiphons are said with the three psalms chosen from the complementary psalmody. If, however, special psalms are to be used or if a solemnity occurs on a Sunday, the psalms are taken from the Sunday of Week I.

83. The complementary psalmody consists of groups of three psalms, usually chosen from the 'gradual' psalms.

VI. Compline

84. Compline is the final prayer of the day to be said before going to bed, even if this is after midnight.

85. Compline, like the other Hours, is begun with the verse *Deus, in adiutorium* with the *Gloria, Sicut erat* and (outside of Lent) the *Alleluia.*

86. It is praiseworthy to follow the introductory verse with an examination of conscience. In common recitation it is made in silence or inserted into one of the penitential acts given in the Roman Missal.

87. A suitable hymn is then said.

88. The psalmody: after first Vespers of Sundays – Ps 4 and Ps 133; after second Vespers of Sundays – Ps 90.

Psalms which evoke confidence in God are chosen for the other days. It is always permissible to substitute these other Psalms with the Sunday psalms on weekdays; this is particularly helpful for those who may want to recite Compline from memory.

89. After the psalmody, there is a short reading and then the responsory *In manus tuas*. Then follows the Gospel canticle the *Nunc dimittis* with its antiphon – the culmination of the whole Hour.

90. The concluding prayer is said as in the Psalter.

91. After the prayer, the blessing *Noctem quietam* is said even in individual recitation.

92. Finally one of the antiphons of the Blessed Virgin Mary is said. In Eastertide this is always the *Regina caeli*. In addition to the antiphons given in *The Liturgy of the Hours*, others may be approved by the Episcopal Conference.[75]

VII. The Way of Joining Hours of the Office with Mass or Among Themselves

93. In special cases, if the circumstances require it, a liturgical Hour celebrated in public or in common may be joined more closely with Mass, provided that they are both of the same Office. This should be done in accord with the norms which follow. Care should be taken to ensure that this is not pastorally harmful, especially on Sundays.

94. When Lauds, celebrated in choir or in common, immediately precedes Mass, the liturgical function may begin either with the introductory verse and hymn of Lauds (especially on ferial days), or with the entrance song and procession, and the celebrant's greeting (especially on festive days). When one of these introductory forms is used, the other is omitted.

The psalmody of Lauds is said in the usual way as far as the short reading exclusively. The penitential act of the Mass is omitted, as also the *Kyrie*, if so desired; the *Gloria in excelsis* is then said, if the rubrics require it, and the celebrant says the collect of the Mass. The Liturgy of the Word follows in the usual way.

The Prayer of the Faithful is said at the normal time and in the form customary at Mass. During the morning Mass of a ferial day, however, the Prayers of Lauds may replace daily formulas of the Prayer of the Faithful.

After the Communion song, the *Benedictus* is sung with its antiphon, followed by the postcommunion prayer and the remainder of Mass as normal.

95. If the public celebration of the Middle Hour, namely Terce, Sext or None, depending on the time of day, immediately precedes Mass, the service may begin with the introductory verse and hymn of the Hour (especially on ferial days), or with the entrance song and procession, and celebrant's greeting (especially on festive days). When one of these introductory forms is used, the other is omitted.

The psalmody of the Hour then follows in the usual way as far as the short reading exclusively Omitting the penitential act and if desired the *Kyrie*, the *Gloria in excelsis* is said if the rubrics require it, and the celebrant says the prayer of the day.

96. Vespers celebrated immediately before Mass is joined with it in the same way as Lauds. First Vespers of solemnities, Sundays and feasts of our Lord occurring on Sundays may not be celebrated until after the Mass of the previous day or the Saturday.

97. When a Middle Hour – Terce, Sext and None – or Vespers follows Mass, the Mass is celebrated in the usual way as far as the postcommunion prayer inclusively.

The psalmody of the Hour begins without an introductory verse immediately after the postcommunion prayer. In a Middle Hour the short reading is omitted after the psalmody, and the concluding prayer said, followed by a dismissal as at Mass. At Vespers, the *Magnificat* with its antiphon follows immediately after the psalmody – there is no reading and no Prayers with the Lord's Prayer – and then comes the concluding prayer and the blessing of the people.

98. Except in the case of Christmas Night, the joining of Mass with the Office of Readings is usually excluded, since the Mass itself has its own sequence of readings differing from that of the Office of Readings. If on a given occasion it is necessary to do this, then Mass begins immediately after the second reading and responsory of this Office, omitting everything before the *Gloria in excelsis* (if this is to be said) or the collect.

99. If the Office of Readings is said immediately before another Hour of the Office, then a hymn fitting to this other Hour may be used to begin the Office of Readings. The prayer and conclusion at the end of the Office of Readings and the introductory verse with the *Gloria Patri* of the succeeding Hour are omitted.

Chapter Three

The Various Parts of the Liturgy of the Hours

I. The Psalms and their Close Relationship with Christian Prayer

100. In the Liturgy of the Hours, the Church for the most part prays with those beautiful songs composed under the inspiration of the Spirit of God by the sacred authors of the Old Testament. From the beginning they have had the power to raise men's minds to God, to evoke in them holy and wholesome thoughts, to help them to give thanks in time of favour, and to bring consolation and constancy in adversity.

101. The psalms offer only a foretaste of the fullness of time revealed in Christ our Lord and from which the prayer of the Church receives its strength; therefore it is not surprising if, even though all Christians agree in having the highest regard for the psalms, difficulty sometimes arises when a person tries to make these songs his own in prayer.

102. The Holy Spirit, who inspired the psalmists, is always present with his grace to those believing Christians who with good intention sing and recite these songs. It is necessary, however, for each according to his powers, to have 'more intensive biblical instruction, especially with regard to the psalms',[1] and be led to see how and in what way he may be able to recite and pray the psalms properly.

103. The psalms are not readings nor were they specifically composed as prayers, but as poems of praise. Though sometimes they may be proclaimed like a reading, nevertheless, because of their literary character, they are rightly called in Hebrew *Tehillim*, that is, 'Songs of Praise', and in Greek *Psalmoi*, 'Songs to be sung to the sound of the harp.' In all the psalms there is a certain musical quality which determines the correct way of praying them. Therefore, though a psalm may be recited without being sung even by an individual in silence, its musical character should not be overlooked. Whilst certainly offering a text to our mind, the psalm is more concerned with moving the spirits of those singing and listening, and indeed of those accompanying it with music.

104. Whoever sings the psalms properly, meditating as he passes from verse to verse, is always prepared to respond in his heart to the movements of that Spirit who inspired the psalmists and is present to devout men and women ready to accept his grace. Thus the psalmody, though it commands the reverence due to the majesty of God, should be conducted in joy and a spirit of charity, as befits the freedom of the children of God, and is in harmony with divinely inspired poetry and song.

105. Often enough the words of the psalm help us to pray easily and fervently: when they express thanksgiving or joyfully bless God, or when they present us with a prayer from the depths of sorrow. On the other hand, especially if the psalm is not addressed to God, we may sometimes find ourselves in difficulties. Because the psalmist is a poet, he often speaks to the people, recalling, for example, the history of Israel; sometimes he addresses others, including those created things which lack the use of reason. He may sometimes write as if God himself and men, and even, as in Ps 2, the enemies of God, are talking to one another. Clearly a psalm has not the same quality of prayer that a prayer or collect composed by the Church may possess. Moreover, since the psalms have a musical and poetic character, they are not necessarily addressed to God, but may be sung before God; St Benedict remarked: 'Let us consider what we should be in the sight of God and angels; we should stand to sing psalms in such a way that our mind is in accord with our voice.'[2]

106. Whoever sings a psalm opens his heart to those emotions which inspired the psalm, each according to its literary type, whether it be a psalm of lament, confidence, thanksgiving or any other type designated by exegetes.

107. The person praying the psalms is conscious of their importance for Christian living by keeping to their literal meaning.

Each psalm was composed in particular circumstances, suggested by the titles which head the psalms in the Hebrew Psalter. But whatever may be said of its historical origin, each psalm has a literal meaning which even in our times cannot be neglected. Though these songs originated many centuries ago in a semitic culture, they express the pain and hope, misery and confidence of men of any age and land, and especially sing of faith in God, his revelation and his redemption.

108. Whoever prays the psalms in the Liturgy of the Hours does not say them in his own name so much as in the name of the whole body of Christ, in fact in the person of Christ himself. If he keeps this in mind, difficulties disappear, even if while saying the psalms his own feelings differ from those expressed by the psalmist: if, for example, we find ourselves saying a psalm of jubilation, while we are worried or sad, or saying a psalm of lament, when in fact we feel in good spirits. This may easily be avoided in merely private prayer, when a psalm can be chosen to suit our mood. In the divine Office, however, even someone saying the Hour alone is not praying the psalms privately but recites them in the name of the Church and according to the sequence given in her public prayer. Whoever says them in the name of the Church, can always find a reason for joy or sorrow, finding applicable to himself the words of the apostle: 'Rejoice with those who rejoice and be sad with those in sorrow' (Rom 12:15); human weakness and selfishness is thus healed by charity so that the mind and heart may harmonize with the voice.[3]

109. Whoever says the psalms in the name of the Church should pay attention to the full meaning of the psalms, especially that messianic understanding which led the Church to adopt the Psalter. The messianic meaning is made completely manifest in the New Testament; it is in fact declared by Christ our Lord himself when he said to the apostles: 'Everything written about me in the Law of Moses, in the prophets and in the psalms, has to be fulfilled' (Luke 24:44). The most notable example of this is the dialogue, in Matthew, about the Messiah; David's Son and Lord is understood, in Ps 109, of the Messiah.[4]

Following this path, the Fathers took the whole Psalter and explained it as a prophecy about Christ and his Church; and for this same reason psalms were chosen for the sacred liturgy. Even if certain artificial interpretations were sometimes accepted, generally both the Fathers and the liturgy rightly heard in the psalms Christ calling out to his Father, or the Father speaking to the Son; they even recognized in them the voice of the Church, the apostles and the martyrs. This method of interpretation also flourished in the Middle Ages; in many manuscripts of the Psalter written at that time, the christological meaning is explained after the heading of each psalm. This christological interpretation in no way refers only to those psalms which are considered messianic but also extends to many in which without doubt there are mere appropriations. Such appropriations, however, have been commended by the tradition of the Church.

Especially in the psalmody of festive days, the psalms are chosen for some christological reason; very often antiphons taken from the psalms themselves are offered to illustrate this.

II. The Antiphons and Other Parts which Help in Praying the Psalms

110. In the Latin tradition three aids are given which greatly assist us to sing the psalms and to turn them into Christian prayer: namely, the headings, the psalm-prayers, and especially the antiphons.

111. In the Psalter of the Liturgy of the Hours, a heading is put before each psalm to indicate its meaning and importance in Christian life. These headings are given in *The Liturgy of the Hours* merely as an aid for the person saying the psalms. To promote prayer in the light of the new revelation, a phrase from the New Testament or Fathers is added as an invitation to pray in a Christian way.

112. Psalm-prayers, which help those reciting the psalms to interpret them in a Christian way, are given for each psalm in a Supplementary Volume of *The Liturgy of the Hours*. These are for optional use in accordance with the traditional norm: when the psalm has been completed and a short silence observed, the psalm-prayer sums up the aspirations and emotions of those saying them.

113. Even when the Liturgy of the Hours is not sung, each psalm has its own antiphon which is also to be said in individual recitation. The antiphons help to illustrate the literary character of the psalm; turn the psalm into personal prayer; place in better light a phrase worthy of attention which may otherwise be missed; give special colour to a psalm in differing circumstances; while excluding arbitrary accommodations, help considerably in the typological and festive interpreting of the psalm; and can make more attractive and varied the recitation of the psalms.

114. The antiphons in the Psalter are drawn up in such a way that they may be translated into the vernacular, and be repeated after each strophe of their psalm, as noted in n. 125. 'Throughout the year', if the Office is not sung, the phrases attached to the psalms may be used instead of these antiphons, if desired (cf. n. 111).

115. When a psalm is long it may be divided into several parts within one and the same Hour. Each part has its own antiphon for the sake of variety, especially in sung celebration. The antiphon also serves to highlight the riches of the psalm. However, one is allowed to complete the psalm without interruption, using only the first antiphon.

116. Proper antiphons are given for each psalm at Lauds and Vespers: in the Paschal Triduum, on the octave days of Easter and Christmas, Sundays of Advent, Christmas, Lent and Easter, and also on the ferial days of Holy Week, Eastertide and December 17–24.

117. On solemnities, at the Office of Readings, Lauds, Terce, Sext, None and Vespers, there are proper antiphons, or, if this is not the case, they are taken from the appropriate Common. On feasts, there are proper antiphons for the Office of Readings, Lauds and Vespers.

118. If some memorials of saints have proper antiphons, these are retained (cf. n. 235).

119. The antiphons at the *Benedictus* and the *Magnificat*, in the Seasonal Office, are taken from the Proper of the Season if there are any, otherwise from the current Psalter. On solemnities and feasts, they are taken from the Proper, otherwise from the Common. On memorials which do not have a proper antiphon, the antiphon may be said either from the Common or from the current ferial day.

120. In Eastertide, *Alleluia* is added to every antiphon, unless its addition clashes with the meaning of the antiphon.

III. The Way of Praying the Psalms

121. The psalms can be recited in various ways taking into account: whether they are said in Latin or in the vernacular, and especially whether they are said by an individual or by a group, or recited in a celebration with the people. A way should be chosen to enable those who pray the psalms to appreciate more easily their spiritual and literary flavour. Psalms are not used just to make up a certain quantity of prayer; a consideration of variety and the character of each enters into their choice.

122. Psalms are sung or said straight through (*in directum*); with alternate verses or strophes sung or recited by two choirs or two parts of the congregation; or in responsorial fashion – the ways tested by tradition and experience.

123. An antiphon is said at the beginning of each psalm (cf. nn. 113–120). The custom of concluding the psalm with *Gloria Patri* and *Sicut erat* is retained. Tradition has aptly employed the *Gloria* to attribute to the prayer of the Old Testament a quality of praise and a christological and trinitarian meaning. The antiphon may, if so desired, be repeated after the psalm.

124. When a longer psalm is used, it is divided up in the Psalter. The divisions are made so that the three-part structure of an Hour's psalmody may be maintained, whilst close attention is paid to the objective meaning of the psalm.

It is best to observe this division, especially in choral celebration in Latin, with the *Gloria Patri* added at the end of each part.

It is permitted either to retain this traditional way, or to pause between the divided parts of the psalm, or to say the whole psalm with its antiphon straight through.

125. The literary character may suggest that the verses of the psalm be indicated and the antiphon repeated after each verse, especially if it is sung in the vernacular. In this case, it is sufficient to put the *Gloria Patri* at the end of the whole psalm.

IV. The Way the Psalms are Distributed in the Office

126. The psalms are distributed over a four-week cycle. In this cycle, a very small number of psalms are omitted, while the traditionally more important ones are repeated more frequently. Lauds, Vespers and Compline have psalms corresponding with their respective Hour.[5]

127. As Lauds and Vespers are designed for celebration with the people, the psalms more suitable for this purpose are chosen for these Hours.

128. At Compline the norm of n. 88 should be observed.

129. On Sundays, even at the Office of Readings and the Middle Hour, psalms are chosen which traditionally express the paschal mystery. Penitential psalms or ones relating to the Passion are assigned to Fridays.

130. Ps 77, Ps 104 and Ps 105 more clearly unfold the way the history of salvation in the Old Testament prefigures its outcome in the New Testament. These three psalms are reserved for Advent, Christmas, Lent and Eastertide.

131. Three psalms are omitted from the current Psalter because of their imprecatory character. These are Ps 57, Ps 82 and Ps 108. For similar reasons verses from several psalms are passed over; these verses are noted at the beginning of the Psalm. Such omissions are made because of certain psychological difficulties, even though the imprecatory psalms themselves may be found quoted in the New Testament, e.g. Apoc 6:10, and in no way are intended to be used as curses.

132. Psalms too long to be included in one Hour of the Office are assigned to the same Hour over several days, so that they may be said in their entirety by those who do not usually say other Hours. Thus Ps 118, traditional for the day Hours, is used for the Middle Hour over twenty-two days, in accordance with its own structure.

133. The Psalter's four-week cycle is joined to the liturgical year in such a way that the First Sunday of Advent, the First Sunday 'thoughout the year', the First Sunday of Lent and Easter Sunday begin the first week of the cycle. Remaining weeks of the cycle before these Sundays are omitted.

After Pentecost, since in time 'throughout the year' the cycle of the Psalter follows the sequence of weeks, it is taken up from that week of the Psalter which is indicated at the beginning of the respective week 'throughout the year' in the Proper of the Season.

134. On solemnities and feasts, during the Paschal Triduum and on the octave days of Easter and Christmas, proper psalms are assigned to the Office of Readings. Their choice is hallowed by tradition and their suitability generally illustrated by the antiphon. The same applies to the Middle Hour on some solemnities of our Lord and in the octave of Easter. At Lauds, the psalms and canticle of Sunday I of the Psalter are used. At first Vespers of solemnities, the psalms, following an old custom, are taken from the *Laudate* series. At second Vespers of solemnities and at Vespers of feasts, the psalms and canticle are proper. At the Middle Hour of solemnities, excepting those already mentioned and when not a Sunday, 'gradual' psalms are chosen; at the Middle Hour of feasts, the psalms are of the current day.

135. In all other cases, the psalms are said from the current Psalter, unless there happen to be proper antiphons or proper psalms.

V. The Canticles of the Old and New Testament

136. At Lauds, it is customary to insert a canticle of the Old Testament between the first and second psalm. Besides the series found in ancient Roman tradition, and the second series introduced into the Breviary by Pope Pius X, many other canticles are added to the Psalter from various books of the Old Testament, so that each ferial day of the four weeks has its own proper canticle; on Sundays, the two parts of the Canticle of the Three Children are used alternately.

137. At Vespers, after the two psalms, a canticle from the Epistles or the Apocalypse of the New Testament is inserted. There are seven such canticles, one for each day of the week. On Sundays of Lent, instead of the Alleluia canticle from the Apocalypse, a canticle from the First Letter of St Peter is said. On the Epiphany and on the feast of the Transfiguration, the canticle is from the First Letter to Timothy.

138. The Gospel canticles, the *Benedictus*, the *Magnificat* and the *Nunc dimittis*, should be accorded the same solemnity and dignity as is usual for the hearing of the Gospel. stand

139. The constant rule of tradition is retained in the arrangement of the psalmody and the readings: first the Old Testament, then the Apostle and finally the proclamation of the Gospel.

VI. The Reading of Sacred Scripture

a. The Reading of Sacred Scripture in General

140. Following ancient tradition, sacred scripture is read publicly in the liturgy not only in the celebration of the Eucharist but also in the Divine Office. This liturgical reading of scripture is of the greatest importance for all Christians because it is offered by the Church herself and not by the decision or whim of a single individual. 'Within the cycle of a year' the mystery of Christ is unfolded by his Bride 'not only from his incarnation and birth until his ascension, but also as reflected in the day of Pentecost, and the expectation of a blessed, hoped-for return of the Lord'.[6] In liturgical celebrations prayer always accompanies the reading of sacred scripture. In this way the reading may bear greater fruit, and conversely prayer, especially through the psalms, may be more fully developed by the reading and encourage more intense devotion.

141. In the Liturgy of the Hours, there may be a longer or a shorter reading of sacred scripture.

142. A longer reading is optional for Lauds and Vespers. This has been described above in n. 46.

b. The Arrangement of the Reading of Sacred Scripture in the Office of Readings

143. The arrangement for the reading of sacred scripture in the Office of Readings has taken account of both the sacred seasons during which certain books are traditionally read, and the sequence of readings at Mass. The reading of scripture in the Liturgy of the Hours is linked with and completes the reading at Mass; in this way the history of salvation is viewed as a whole.

144. With the exception made in n. 73, the Gospel is not read in the Liturgy of the Hours. The whole of it is read each year during Mass.

145. There is a twofold arrangement for the biblical readings. The first lasts for one year; it is found in *The Liturgy of the Hours*. The second, for optional use, is found in the *Supplement*; this, like the arrangement of first readings in ferial Masses 'throughout the year', is arranged in a two-year cycle.

146. This biennial arrangement, assigned to the Liturgy of the

Hours, allows the inclusion every year of nearly all the books of sacred scripture, as also the long and difficult passages which scarcely have a place in the Mass. The whole of the New Testament is read every year, partly at Mass and partly in the Liturgy of the Hours. Passages from the Old Testament books are chosen for their greater importance in the understanding of the history of salvation and for their devotional value.

Due harmony between the readings of the Liturgy of the Hours and the readings of Mass necessarily demands that passages from the same biblical book recur in alternate years in the Missal and in the Office, or at least if read in the same year, there be some space of time between the reading at Mass and the reading in the Hours. This is to prevent the same texts occuring on the same days in both, or the same books being distributed over the same time, thus leaving the Liturgy of the Hours with passages of less importance or upsetting the series of texts.

147. During Advent, following ancient tradition, passages from the book of Isaiah are read semi-continuously on a two-yearly basis. The book of Ruth is also added and certain prophecies from the book of Micah. Since there are special readings assigned for 17–24 December, the readings of the third week of Advent which remain unused are omitted.

148. From 29 December until 5 January: in Year I of the cycle there are readings from the Letter to the Colossians, in which the Incarnation of the Lord is considered in the context of the whole history of salvation; in Year II, it is the Song of Songs, in which is foreshadowed the union of God and man in Christ: 'God the Father prepared a marriage for God the Son, when he united him with human nature in the Virgin's womb, when God living before all ages wanted to become man to the end of all ages.'[7]

149. From 7 January until the Saturday after the Epiphany, eschatological texts from Isaiah 60–66 and Baruch are read; texts remaining unused are omitted that year.

150. In Lent: in Year I passages from the book of Deuteronomy and the Letter to the Hebrews are read; in Year II, attention is directed to the history of salvation as found in the books of Exodus, Leviticus and Numbers. The Letter to the Hebrews interprets the old covenant in the light of the paschal mystery of Christ. From this Letter, the passage concerning the sacrifice of Christ is read on Good Friday, and the text about God's place of 'Rest' on Holy Saturday.

On the other days of Holy Week: in Year I, the third and fourth songs of the Servant of God and passages from the book of Lamentations are read; in Year II, we hear the prophet Jeremiah, the type of the suffering Christ.

151. In Eastertide, except on Sundays 1 & 2 of Easter and the solemnities of the Ascension and Pentecost: in accordance with tradition, in Year I, the First Letter of St Peter, the Letters of St John and the Apocalypse are read; during Year II, the Acts of the Apostles.

152. From the Monday after the Baptism of our Lord until Lent, and from the Monday after Pentecost until Advent, there is a continuous series of thirty-four weeks 'throughout the year'.

This series is interrupted from Ash Wednesday until Pentecost Day. On the Monday after Pentecost, the readings are taken up from the week 'throughout the year' which follows the week interrupted by Lent, omitting the readings assigned to the Sunday of that week.

In years which have only thirty-three weeks 'throughout the year', the week which comes immediately after Pentecost is omitted, so that the readings with an eschatalogical character set for the final weeks 'throughout the year' are always heard.

The sequence of Old Testament books follows the history of salvation: God led and enlightened his people step by step revealing himself in the course of its life. Thus the prophets are read in between the historical books, taking into account the time in which they lived and taught. In Year I the series of Old Testament readings offers the historical books together with the prophetic books from the book of Joshua to the time of the Exile inclusively. In Year II readings before Lent are from Genesis, and then the history of salvation is recounted from the Exile until the time of the Maccabees. The later prophets, the wisdom books and the narrative books of Esther, Tobit and Judith have their place in Year II.

The Letters of the Apostles not read at special times are distributed over other periods, taking account of the readings at Mass and the chronological order in which they were written.

153. The single year arrangement is abbreviated in such a way that every year passages are selected complementary to the two-year sequence of scripture readings at Mass.

154. Solemnities and feasts have proper readings, otherwise they are taken from the Common of Saints.

155. Each passage forms a unity in so far as this is possible. Thus verses are sometimes left out to retain a suitable length, which can vary according to the different literary characters of the books – omitted verses are always indicated.

c. Short readings

156. The importance of short readings or 'chapters' in the Liturgy of the Hours has been noted in n. 45. They are selected to express briefly and succinctly a biblical phrase, theme or exhortation, and have been chosen with an eye to variety.

157. A four-week cycle of short readings 'throughout the year' has been introduced into the Psalter, so as to vary the reading every day for four weeks. For Advent, Christmas, Lent and Eastertide, the variation is on a single-week basis. There are proper short readings for solemnities, feasts and certain memorials, and a single-week series for Compline.

158. In the selection of short readings, the following have been kept in mind:

a) the Gospels have been excluded, as is traditional;

b) the character of Sunday, Friday and the Hours themselves has been taken into account;

c) the short readings at Vespers are chosen from the New Testament, given that they follow a New Testament canticle.

VII. The Readings from the Fathers and Church Writers

159. According to the tradition of the Roman Church, the biblical passage in the Office of Readings is followed by a reading from the Fathers or Church writers with a responsory, unless a hagiographical reading is to be said (cf. nn. 228–239).

160. In this reading texts are offered from the writings of the Fathers, Doctors and other Church writers from the East and the West. Pride of place is given to the Fathers, who enjoy special authority in the Church.

161. Besides the readings assigned to each day in *The Liturgy of the Hours*, there is an optional Lectionary. This offers a much larger collection of readings in which the treasures of the Church's tradition are opened more widely to those praying the Divine Office. One is allowed to take the second reading either from *The Liturgy of the Hours* or from the optional Lectionary.

162. Episcopal Conferences may prepare other additional texts which are in harmony with the traditions and mentality of their own area; these texts may form a supplement to the optional Lectionary. They should be taken from the works of Catholic writers outstanding for their teaching and holiness of life.[8]

163. The purpose of this reading is above all to offer a meditation on the word of God as it has been accepted in the Church's tradition. The Church has always felt it necessary to give the faithful an authentic interpretation of the word of God, so that 'prophetic and apostolic interpretation may be guided in a Catholic and ecclesial way'.[9]

164. By constant use of writings drawn from the tradition of the universal Church, readers are led to a deeper meditation on sacred scripture and to a more lively appreciation of it. The writings of the Fathers are outstanding witnesses of the reflexion on the word of God which the Church, the Bride of the Incarnate Word, has continued down the centuries. 'She possesses in herself the understanding and spirit of her Bridegroom and God,'[10] and daily learns to advance towards a deeper penetration of the sacred scriptures.

165. The reading of the Fathers also teaches Christians the meaning of the seasons and feasts. It opens to them the incalculable spiritual riches which constitute the noble heritage of the Church. At the same time it gives foundation to the spiritual life and abundant nourishment to devotion. Thus preachers of the word of God have daily set before them excellent examples of sacred preaching.

VIII. The Hagiographical Reading

166. The name 'hagiographical reading' refers to: a text of a Father or Church writer who actually speaks of the saint being honoured or says something which may be correctly applied to him; an excerpt from the writings of the saint himself; or an account of his life.

167. In composing the special Propers of the Saints, emphasis should be given to historical truth[11] and to the spiritual benefit of those who read or hear the hagiographical reading. Writings which merely seek to impress should be scrupulously avoided. The particular spiritual qualities of the saints should be highlighted, bearing in mind today's conditions, as also their importance in the life and spirituality of the Church.

168. A short biographical note, giving just historical information and describing briefly the saint's life, is placed before each reading. It is for information only, and should not be read out in the celebration.

IX. The Responsories

169. The biblical reading in the Office of Readings is followed by its own responsory. The text of this response, chosen from traditional material or newly composed, is designed to cast new light on the passage just read, to place the reading within the history of salvation, to draw it from the Old Testament into the New, to turn the reading to prayer and contemplation, or finally to offer further variety and beauty.

170. In a similar way a suitable response is given to the second reading. This, however, is not so strictly linked with the text of the reading, and thus favours greater freedom of meditation.

171. The responsories, with their parts to be repeated, retain their value even in individual recitation. The part usually repeated in the responsory may be omitted if not sung, unless repetition is demanded by its very meaning.

172. In a similar but simpler way, the brief responsory at Lauds, Vespers and Compline (about which see nn. 49 & 89 above), and the versicles at Terce, Sext and None, reply to the short reading. This brief response is a kind of acclamation, and enables the word of God to penetrate more deeply into the mind and heart of the person reciting or listening.

X. The Hymns and other Non-Biblical Songs

173. Hymns have a place in the Office from very early times, a position they continue to retain.[12] Not only does their lyrical nature make them specially suited to the praise of God, but they constitute a popular part, since nearly always they point more immediately than the other parts of the Office to the individual characteristics of the Hours or of each feast. They help to move the people taking part and draw them into the celebration. Their literary beauty often increases their effectiveness. In the Office, the hymns are the principal poetic part composed by the Church.

174. The hymn is traditionally concluded by a doxology, which is usually addressed to the same divine person as the hymn itself.

175. For the sake of variety in the Office 'throughout the year', there are two series of hymns for each Hour, to be used on alternate weeks.

176. In the Office of Readings, there are two series of hymns in time 'throughout the year', depending on whether this Office is recited at night or during the day.

177. New hymns can be given melodies of the same rhythm and metre as the traditional ones.

178. With regard to celebrations in the vernacular, Episcopal Conferences may adapt the Latin hymns to the nature of their own language. They may also introduce new compositions,[13] provided they suit the spirit of the Hour, season or feast; one should constantly beware of permitting those popular songs which are of no artistic value and completely unworthy of the liturgy.

XI. The Prayers, the Lord's Prayer and the Concluding Prayer

a. The Prayer or Intercessions at Lauds and Vespers

179. The Liturgy of the Hours celebrates the praises of God. However, neither Jewish nor Christian tradition separates praise of God from prayer of petition, petition often being drawn out of praise. The apostle Paul advises that 'there should be prayers offered for everyone – petitions, intercessions and thanksgiving – and especially for kings and others in authority, so that we may be able to live religious and reverent lives in peace and quiet. To do this is right, and will please God our saviour: he wants everyone to be saved and reach full knowledge of the truth' (I Timothy 2:1–4). This exhortation was frequently interpreted by the Fathers in the sense that intercessions should be made morning and evening.[14]

180. The Intercessions which have been restored to the Mass of the Roman Rite are also found at Vespers, though, as described below, in a different way.

181. Since traditionally prayer is offered in the morning to commend the whole day to God, invocations are given at Lauds to consecrate the day to him.

182. The name 'Prayers' is applied both to the intercessions made at Vespers, and to the invocations dedicating the day to God made at Lauds.

183. For the sake of variety, but above all that the needs of the Church and mankind may be better expressed according to the different states, groups, persons, conditions and times, different formulas of Prayers are proposed for each day in the arrangement of the Psalter and for the sacred seasons of the liturgical year, as also for certain festive celebrations.

184. Episcopal Conferences have the right to adapt the formulas of *The Liturgy of the Hours* and approve new Prayers,[15] keeping however the following norms.

185. As in the Lord's Prayer, petitions should be linked with praise of God or acknowledgement of his glory, or with the recalling of the history of salvation.

186. In the Prayers of Vespers, the final intention is always for the dead.

187. Since the Liturgy of the Hours is above all the prayer of the whole Church for the whole Church, indeed for the salvation of the whole world,[16] general intentions should always have first place, whether the prayer is for the Church and all her members, for the secular authorities, for those who suffer poverty, disease or sorrow, or for the needs of the whole world, namely, for peace and for other things of this sort.

188. It is permissible to add special intentions at Lauds and Vespers.

189. The Prayers of the Office have a structure adaptable for celebration with the people, for celebration in a small community, or for recitation individually.

190. Prayers for recitation with the people or in common are introduced with a short invitation by the priest or minister. This introduction also includes a phrase or response which the congregation can then repeat after each of the intentions.

191. The intentions should be addressed to God in such a way that they can accord with common celebration or individual recitation.

192. Each intention consists of two parts, the second of which can be used as a variable response.

193. The different methods of saying the Prayers are thus: the priest or minister says both parts of the intention and the congregation adds the invariable response, or pauses for silence; otherwise the priest or minister says only the first part and the congregation the second part of the intention.

b. The Lord's Prayer

194. In accordance with tradition, the Lord's Prayer has the place of honour at the end of the Prayers at the more popular Hours of Lauds and Vespers.

195. The Lord's Prayer will henceforward be solemnly recited three times a day; that is, at Mass, Lauds and Vespers.

196. The Lord's Prayer is said by all, preceded if desired by a brief introduction.

c. The concluding Prayer

197. A concluding Prayer completes the whole Hour. In public celebration with the people, it traditionally pertains to the priest or deacon.[17]

198. This Prayer, in the Office of Readings, is normally the collect of the Mass. At Compline it is always from the Psalter.

199. At Lauds and Vespers, the concluding Prayer is taken from the Proper, on Sundays, ferial days of Advent, Christmas, Lent and Eastertide, as also on solemnities, feasts and memorials. On ferial days 'throughout the year', the Prayer given in the Psalter is said in order to emphasize the particular character of these Hours.

200. At Terce, Sext and None, or at the Middle Hour, the Prayer is taken from the Proper on Sundays, ferial days of Advent, Christmas, Lent and Eastertide, and on solemnities and feasts. On other days concluding Prayers are said which express the character of each Hour; these are found in the Psalter.

XII. The Sacred Silence

201. Since as a general rule in liturgical functions care must be taken that 'at the proper times all should observe a reverent silence',[18] opportunity for silence should be given in the recitation of the Liturgy of the Hours.

202. The purpose of this silence is to allow the voice of the Holy Spirit to be heard more fully in our hearts, and to unite our personal prayer more closely with the word of God and the public voice of the Church. In introducing silence we must use prudence; periods of silence may be inserted in different ways: after the psalm, once its antiphon has been repeated, as was generally the custom, and especially if there is a Psalm-prayer after the silence (cf. n. 112); after the reading whether long or short; either before or after the responsory.

Care should be taken that such a silence neither deforms the structure of the Office, nor upsets or bores the participants.

203. In individual recitation, we have more opportunity to pause and meditate on a text which strikes us. The Office will not lose its public character because of this.

Chapter Four

Various Celebrations in the Course of the Year

I. The Celebration of the Mysteries of the Lord

a. Sundays

204. The Sunday Office begins with first Vespers, in which everything is taken from the Psalter, except for those things which are given as proper.

205. When a feast of the Lord is celebrated on a Sunday, it has its own first Vespers.

206. On the manner of celebrating Sunday vigils when desired, cf. n. 73.

207. It is especially fitting, where it can be done, that, in accordance with ancient custom, at least Vespers be celebrated with the people.[1]

b. The Pascal Triduum

208. During the Paschal Triduum, the Office is celebrated as described in the Proper of the season.

209. Those who participate in the celebration of evening Mass on Holy Thursday or in the celebration of the Passion of the Lord on Good Friday, do not say the Vespers of the respective day.

210. Before morning Lauds on Good Friday and Holy Saturday, the Office of Readings is, if possible, to be celebrated publicly and with the participation of the people.

211. The Compline of Holy Saturday is only said by those who are not present at the Easter Vigil.

212. The Easter Vigil takes the place of the Office of Readings: those not present at the Vigil should therefore choose from it at least four readings with canticles and prayers. It would be appropriate to choose the readings of Exodus, Ezekiel, the Apostle and the Gospel. The *Te Deum* and the prayer of the day follow.

213. On Easter Sunday Lauds are said by all; it is fitting that Vespers should be celebrated in a more solemn manner to mark the close of this holy day and to commemorate the apparitions in which our Lord showed himself to his disciples. The tradition of celebrating Baptismal Vespers, where it is the custom, should be most carefully preserved, in which the procession to the font takes place while the psalms are sung.

c. EASTERTIDE

214. The Liturgy of the Hours receives its paschal character from the *Alleluia* acclamation with which most antiphons conclude (cf. n. 120). This quality is also given by the hymns, antiphons, and special prayers, and finally by the proper readings assigned to each Hour.

d. CHRISTMAS

215. Before the Midnight Mass of Christmas it is appropriate that solemn vigil should be celebrated with the Office of Readings. Compline is not said by those who are present at this vigil.

216. Lauds on Christmas Day are usually said before the Dawn Mass.

e. OTHER SOLEMNITIES AND FEASTS OF OUR LORD

217. As regards the arrangement of the Office on solemnities and feasts of our Lord, what is said in nn. 225–233 should be observed, with the appropriate changes.

II. The Celebration of the Saints

218. The celebrations of the saints are arranged in such a way that they do not take precedence over the mysteries of salvation as commemorated on festive days and during the major seasons of the year,[2] and so that they do not continually interfere with the sequence of the psalms and readings, or give rise to unnecessary repetitions. The purpose of this is also to give everyone ample opportunity for legitimate devotion. The reform of the Liturgical Calendar, undertaken by the Second Vatican Council, is based on these principles, as is the manner of celebrating the saints in the Liturgy of the Hours; this will be described in the following articles.

219. Celebrations of the saints are either solemnities, feasts or memorials.

220. The memorials are either obligatory, or, if nothing to the contrary is indicated, optional. The decision whether or not to celebrate with the faithful or in common the Office of an optional memorial should depend on the common good and devotion of the group and not on the person presiding.

221. If several optional memorials occur on the same day, only one is to be celebrated and the others omitted.

222. Only solemnities are transferable, and this is done in accordance with the rubrics.

223. The norms which follow apply both to the saints of the General Roman Calendar, and to those found in particular calendars.

224. If the Propers are not complete, the Commons of the Saints are used for the parts which are lacking.

1. How the Office is Arranged on Solemnities

225. Solemnities have first Vespers on the preceding day.

226. At first and second Vespers, the hymn, antiphons, short reading with its responsory and the concluding prayer are all proper; if the proper is not complete, the common is used for the parts that are lacking.

Both Psalms in first Vespers are normally taken from the *Laudate* series (that is, Ps 112, 116, 134, 145, 146, 147), in accordance with ancient tradition. The New Testament canticle is indicated in the appropriate place. In second Vespers the psalms and the canticle are proper. The Prayers are either proper or else from the Common.

227. At Lauds, the hymn, antiphons, short reading with its responsory and the concluding prayer are proper; if the proper is lacking, they are taken from the Common. The psalms, however, are to be taken from Sunday I of the Psalter. The Prayers are either proper or else from the Common.

228. In the Office of Readings, everything is proper: the hymns, antiphons and psalms, the readings and responsories. The first reading is biblical, the second hagiographical. In the Office of a saint whose cult is only local and which does not have special texts even in the local Proper, everything is taken from the Common.

At the end of the Office of Readings, the *Te Deum* is said and the proper Prayer.

229. In the Middle Hour, or Terce, Sext and None, the hymn of the ferial day is said, unless otherwise indicated; the 'gradual' psalms are used with a proper antiphon; on Sundays, the psalms are taken from Sunday I of the Psalter, the short reading and the concluding Prayer are proper. On certain solemnities of the Lord special psalms are given.

230. At Compline, everything is from the Sunday, after first and second Vespers respectively.

2. How the Office is Arranged on Feasts

231. Feasts do not have first Vespers, unless they are feasts of the Lord occuring on Sundays. At the Office of Readings, Lauds and Vespers, everything is the same as on a solemnity.

232. In the Middle Hour, or Terce, Sext and None, the hymn of the day is said; the psalms with their antiphons are of the ferial day, unless a special reason or tradition requires that the antiphon at the Middle Hour be proper. This will be indicated in the appropriate place. The short reading and the concluding prayer are from the Proper.

233. Compline is said as on ordinary days.

3. How the Office is Arranged on the Memorials of Saints

234. There is no difference in the manner of arranging the Office between an obligatory memorial, and, if it is decided to celebrate it, an optional memorial, except when the optional memorial occurs during the privileged seasons.

a) *Memorials occuring on ordinary days*

235. In the Office of Readings, and at Lauds and Vespers:

a) the psalms with their antiphons are taken from the current ferial day, unless there are proper antiphons or psalms, as will be indicated in each case;

b) if the antiphon for the invitatory, the hymn, short reading, antiphons at the *Benedictus* and the *Magnificat*, and the prayers are proper, they are to be taken from the Office of the Saint. Otherwise they are taken either from the Common or from the current ferial day;

c) the concluding prayer is to be taken from the Office of the saint;

d) in the Office of Readings, the biblical reading with its responsory is taken from the scripture given for the ferial day.

The second reading is hagiographical, with the responsory either proper or from the Common. If this second reading is not proper it is taken from the patristic text for the current ferial day.

The *Te Deum* is not said.

236. At the Middle Hour, or Terce, Sext and None, and at Compline, nothing is taken from the Office of the Saint but everything from the ferial day.

b) Memorials occuring during the privileged seasons

237. On Sundays, solemnities and feasts, on Ash Wednesday, during Holy Week and the octave of Easter, no memorials are commemorated should they occur.

238. On the ferial days between 17 and 24 December, during the octave of Christmas and on the ferial days of Lent, no obligatory memorials may be celebrated, not even in particular calendars. The memorials which happen to occur during Lent are considered optional memorials for that year.

239. If anyone wishes to celebrate the Office of a saint whose memorial occurs during these seasons:

a) in the Office of Readings, after the patristic reading with its responsory from the Proper of the season, he should add the proper hagiographical reading with its responsory and conclude with the Prayer of the saint;

b) after the concluding prayer at Lauds and Vespers, he may add the antiphon (proper or else from the Common) and Prayer of the saint.

c) The memorial of the Blessed Virgin Mary on Saturdays

240. On Saturdays 'throughout the year' on which optional memorials are permitted, an optional memorial of the Blessed Virgin Mary with its proper reading may be celebrated in the same way.

III. The Use of the Calendar and Choosing an Office or Part of an Office

a. The use of the Calendar

241. The Office in choir or in common is celebrated in accordance with a proper calendar, that is, of the diocese, religious family or individual Churches.[3] Members of religious families are to join with the community of the local church in celebrating the dedication of the cathedral church, and the principal patrons of the place and of the region in which they live.[4]

242. A cleric or religious bound in any way to the recitation of the divine Office who participates in the celebration of the Office in common according to a calendar or rite other than his own satisfies in this way his obligation for that part of the Office.

243. In individual celebration, either the calendar of the place or a proper calendar may be used except on proper solemnities and feasts.[5]

b. The Choice of an Office

244. On ferial days which admit the celebration of an optional memorial the Office of a particular saint, who is included for that day in the Roman Martyrology or in its approved Appendix may, for a good reason, be celebrated in the normal way (cf. nn. 234–239).

245. Except on solemnities, Sundays of Advent, Lent and Easter, Ash Wednesday, during Holy Week and the octave of Easter, and on 2 November, a votive Office may be celebrated either whole or in part for a public or devotional reason: for example, at the time of a pilgrimage, on a local feast, or during the external solemnity of a saint.

c. The Choice of Texts

246. Provided that the general arrangement of each Hour is maintained and that the rules which follow are observed, texts other than those found in the Office of the day may be chosen on particular occasions.

247. In the Office of Sundays, solemnities, feasts of the Lord which are in the General Calendar, on ferial days of Lent and Holy Week, on octave days of Easter and Christmas, and on the ferial days between 17 and 24 December inclusive, it is never permitted to change the texts which are proper or appropriated to the celebration. These include the antiphons, hymns, readings, responsories, prayers, and, very often, the psalms.

In place of the Sunday psalms of the current week, the Sunday psalms of another week may be substituted if desired. Especially in the Office with the people, other psalms may be chosen so as gradually to bring the people to a deeper understanding of the Psalter.

248. In the Office of Readings, the continuous reading of scripture should always be highly regarded. The wish of the Church that 'a more representative portion of the holy scriptures will be read to the people over a set cycle of years'[6] also applies to the Office.

Therefore, the sequence of scripture readings given in the Office of Readings for Advent, Christmas, Lent and Easter, should be maintained; in time 'throughout the year' for a good reason, on a given day or for a few successive days, the readings may be selected from among those given for other days or even from other readings of the scriptures, for example, during retreats, pastoral gatherings, times of prayer for Christian unity and other things of this kind.

249. If the continuous readings are interrupted because of a solemnity, feast, or special celebration, in the same week it is permissible, taking into account the sequence for the whole week, either to join the passages to be omitted with the ones remaining, or to decide which texts are to be preferred.

250. Likewise in the Office of Readings, instead of the second reading assigned to a particular day, if there is a good reason, another reading may be chosen from the same season, taken either from *The Liturgy of the Hours* or from the optional Lectionary (n. 161). Furthermore, on ferial days 'throughout the year', and, if it seems suitable, even during Advent, Christmas, Lent and Easter, a quasi-continuous reading may be taken from a work of one of the Fathers. This work should be in harmony with the spirit of the bible and the liturgy.

251. The readings, collects, songs and prayers, given for Lauds, Vespers and the other Hours of ferial days during a particular season, may be said on other ferial days of the same season, except in those cases indicated in n. 247.

252. Even though everyone should be concerned to observe the four-week cycle of the Psalter,[7] for a good spiritual or pastoral reason, instead of the psalms assigned to a particular day other psalms may be said which are found in the same Hour of a different day. Sometimes circumstances arise in which it is permissible to choose suitable psalms and other parts as for a votive Office.

Chapter Five

The Rites to be Observed in Communal Celebration

I. The Various Tasks to be Performed

253. In the celebration of the Liturgy of the Hours as in other liturgical actions 'whether as a minister or as one of the faithful, each person should perform his role by doing solely and totally what the nature of things and liturgical norms require of him'.[1]

254. When the bishop presides, especially in his cathedral church, it is desirable that his priests and ministers should gather round him, together with the full and active participation of the faithful. In every celebration with the people, a priest or deacon should normally preside, and there should also be ministers present.

255. The priest or deacon who presides at the ceremony may wear a stole over his alb or surplice. The priest can also wear a cope. On the major solemnities there is nothing to prevent several priests wearing copes and the deacons dalmatics.

256. It is the role of the presiding priest or deacon, from the seat, to begin the Office with the introductory verse, to begin the Lord's Prayer, say the Concluding Prayer, greet, bless and dismiss the people.

257. Either the priest or a minister may say the Prayers.

258. When there is no priest or deacon, the person who presides is only one among equals; he does not enter the sanctuary, nor does he greet or bless the people.

259. The lector should stand in a suitable place to proclaim the readings, whether these are long or short.

260. A cantor or cantors should begin the antiphons, psalms and other songs. With regard to the psalmody, the norms of nn. 121–125 should be observed.

261. During the Gospel canticle at Lauds and Vespers, the altar may be incensed, and then also the priest and people.

262. The obligation to choir pertains to the community and not to the place of celebration. This need not necessarily be a church, especially if it is a question of those Hours which are recited without solemnity.

263. All participants stand:

a) during the introduction to the Office and the introductory verse of each Hour;

b) during the hymn;

c) during the Gospel canticle;

d) during the Prayers, Lord's Prayer and Concluding Prayer.

264. Except during the Gospel, everyone is seated while listening to the readings.

265. While the psalms and other songs with their antiphons are being said, the community sits or stands according to custom.

266. Everyone makes the sign of the cross from the forehead to the breast and from the left shoulder to the right;

a) at the beginning of the Hours, when the *Deus, in adiutorium* is said;

b) at the beginning of the Gospel canticles, the *Benedictus*, the *Magnificat*, and the *Nunc Dimittis*

Everyone makes the sign of the cross on the mouth at the beginning of the invitatory, when saying the words *Domine, labia mea aperies.*

II. Singing in the Office

267. In the rubrics and norms of this Instruction, the words 'say' and 'recite' should be understood as referring to singing or saying in accordance with the principles given below.

268. 'The sung celebration of the divine Office is the form which best accords with the nature of this prayer. It expresses its solemnity in a fuller way and expresses a deeper union of hearts in performing the praises of God. That is why, in accordance with the wish of the Constitution on the Liturgy, this sung form is strongly recommended to those who celebrate the Office in choir or in common.'[2]

269. What the Second Vatican Council said with regard to singing in the Liturgy applies to every liturgical action but especially to the Liturgy of the Hours.[3] Although each and every part has been so arranged that it can fruitfully be recited even by an individual, many of them, especially the psalms, canticles, hymns and responsories, are of a lyrical nature and are given their full expression only when sung.

270. Singing in the Liturgy of the Hours is not to be regarded as something merely ornamental or extrinsic to prayer. It springs from the depths of the person praying and praising God, and fully and perfectly reveals the communal character of Christian worship.

To be commended therefore are those Christian communities – whatever their character – which endeavour as often as possible to use this form of praying the Office. Clerics, religious and faithful should be given proper instruction and practice in the singing of the Office, so that especially on festive days they will be able to enjoy singing the Hours. However difficult it is to sing the whole Office, the praise of the Church is not to be considered either in its origins or of its nature as the preserve of clerics and monks; it belongs to the whole Christian community. Many principles are to be borne in mind if the singing of the Liturgy of the Hours is to be carried out correctly, and if its value and beauty are to be appreciated.

271. It is especially appropriate that singing should be used at least on Sundays and festive days. From this the various degrees of solemnity may be recognized.

272. Not all the Hours are of the same importance. Hence it is fitting that the singing of those Hours which form the two hinges of the Office, namely Lauds and Vespers, should be preferred and solemnized more than the others.

273. Even if a celebration in which everything is sung is to be commended, provided it is of genuine artistic and spiritual value, sometimes the principle of 'progressive' solemnity may be fruitfully employed. This principle may need to be applied for practical reasons, but also because the various parts of the liturgical celebration are not of equal importance. This will mean that each part may again recover its original meaning and purpose. The Liturgy of the Hours should not be looked on as a beautiful monument of a past age, to be preserved almost unchanged in order to excite our admiration. On the contrary, it should come to life again with new meaning and grow to become once more the sign of a living community.

Therefore, the principle of 'progressive' solemnity is one which admits several intermediate stages between the singing of the Office in its entirety and the simple recitation of all its parts.

This principle offers considerable variety, and thus makes the Office more attractive. The measure of this variety is to be judged according to the quality of the day or Hour which is being celebrated, the purpose of the various parts which make up the Office, the number and character of the community, as well as the number of available singers.

This greater degree of variation will allow the public praise of the Church to be sung more frequently than before, and to be better adapted to differing circumstances. We may confidently hope that new ways and new forms may be found for our own age, as has always happened in the Life of the Church.

274. In liturgical celebrations sung in Latin, Gregorian Chant, as proper to the Roman Liturgy, should be given pride of place, other things being equal.[4] In sung Office, if the melody for an antiphon is lacking another antiphon may be taken from the existing repertoire, provided this is in agreement with the norms in nn. 113, 121–125. 'No kind of sacred music is prohibited from liturgical actions by the Church as long as it corresponds to the spirit of the liturgical celebration itself and the nature of its individual parts, and does not hinder the active participation of the people.'[5]

275. Since the Liturgy of the Hours may be celebrated in the vernacular, 'due care should be taken that melodies are prepared which may be used in the singing of the divine Office in the vernacular'.[6]

276. There is nothing to prevent different parts in one and the same celebration being sung in different languages.[7]

277. Which parts should especially be sung depends on what is the best way of arranging the liturgical celebration. This demands that the meaning and proper nature of each part and of each song be carefully observed; some parts require to be sung by their very nature.[8] These are above all: the acclamations, the responses to the greetings of the priest and ministers and the prayers of litany form, and also the antiphons and psalms, refrains or repeated responses, hymns and canticles.[9]

278. Jewish and Christian tradition confirms that the psalms are closely connected with music. To understand many of the psalms fully it helps a great deal to sing them or at least to regard them from a poetic and musical point of view. If possible, this form is to be preferred, at least on the more important days and Hours, while respecting the original character of the psalms.

279. The different ways of reciting the psalms are described above, nn. 121–123. Variety is introduced not because of external circumstances but on account of the various types of psalms which occur in any one celebration. Thus it may be better to say sapiential and historical psalms, while the hymns and psalms of thanksgiving are best sung. It is very important for us to be concerned with the meaning and spirit of what we are doing. The celebration should not be rigid or artificial, nor should we be merely concerned with formalities. Above all, the thing to be achieved is to instil a desire for the authentic prayer  of the Church and a delight in celebrating the praise of God (cf. Ps 146).

280. The hymns, provided they have doctrinal and artistic value, can also be of benefit to the person reciting the Hours. As far as possible, hymns should be sung in community celebration as their nature demands.

281. The short responsory after the reading at Lauds and at Vespers, cf. n. 49, is, by its nature, designed to be sung in common.

282. The nature and purpose of the responsories in the Office of Readings require that they should be sung. They are so composed, however, that even in individual recitation they retain their value. Singing may be used more often for the responsories which have simpler and easier melodies, than for those which are taken from the liturgical sources.

283. The readings, whether they are long or short, are not of themselves intended to be sung. Great care should be taken to proclaim the readings worthily, clearly and distinctly so that they may be easily heard and understood by all. If therefore they are sung, only a form of music which enables them to be better heard and understood may be used.

284. It may be fitting for the president to sing the texts which are to be proclaimed by him alone, such as the prayers, especially if these are in Latin. This may be more difficult in certain vernacular languages, unless singing helps everyone to hear the text more clearly.

Notes

Chapter One

1. Cf. Acts 1:14; 4:24; 12:5, 12; cf. Eph 5:19–21.
2. Cf. Acts 2:1–15.
3. Second Vatican Council, *Const. on the Sacred Liturgy*, *Sacrosanctum Concilium*, n. 83. (English Translation: *The Documents of Vatican II*, edited by W. M. Abbott, S. J. and Joseph Gallagher.)
4. Lk 3:21–22.
5. Lk 6:12.
6. Mt 14:19; 15:36; Mk 6:41; 8:7; Lk 9:16; John 6:11.
7. Lk 9:28–29.
8. Mk 7:34.
9. John 11:41ff.
10. Lk 9:18.
11. Lk 11:1.
12. Mt 11:25ff; Lk 10:21ff.
13. Mt 19:13.
14. Lk 22:32.
15. Mk 1:35; 6:46; Lk 5:16; cf. Mt 4:1 par.; Mt 14:23.
16. Mk 1:35.
17. Lk 6:12.
18. Mt 14:23, 25; Mk 6:46, 48.
19. Lk 4:16.
20. Mt 21:13 par.
21. Mt 14:19 par, Mt 15:36 par.
22. Mt 26:26 par.
23. Lk 24:30.
24. Mt 26:30 par.
25. John 12:27f.
26. John 17:1–26.
27. Mt 26:36–44 par.
28. Lk 23:34, 46; Mt 27:46; Mk 15:34.
29. Cf. Heb 7:25.
30. Mt 5-44; 7:7; 26:41; Mk 13:33; 14:38; Lk 6:28; 10:2; 11:9; 22:40, 46.
31. John 14:13f; 15:16; 16:23f, 26.
32. Mt 6:9–13; Lk 11:2–4.
33. Lk 18:1.
34. Lk 18:9–14.
35. Lk 21:36; Mk 13:33.
36. Lk 11:5–13; 18:1–8; John 14:13; 16:23.
37. Mt 6:5–8; 23:14; Lk 20:47; John 4:23.
38. Heb 13:15.
39. 2 Cor 1:20; Col 3:17.
40. Rom 8:15, 26; 1 Cor 12:3; Gal 4:6; Jude 20.
41. Rom 12:12; 1 Cor 7:5; Eph 6:18; Col 4:2; 1 Th 5:17; I Tim 5:5; 1 Peter 4:7.
42. 1 Tim 4:5; James 5:15f; 1 John 3:22; 5:14s.
43. Eph 5:19s; Heb 13:15; Apoc 19:5.
44. Col 3:17; Phil 4:6; 1 Th 5:17; 1 Tim 2:1.
45. Rom 8:26; Phil 4:6.
46. Rom 15:30; 1 Tim 2:1s; Eph 6:18; 1 Th 5:25; James 5:14, 16.
47. 1 Tim 2:5; Heb 8:6; 9:15; 12:24.

48. Rom 5:2; Eph 2:18; 3:12.

49. Cf. Second Vatican Council, *Const. on Sacred Liturgy, Sacrosanctum Concilium*, n. 83.

50. Second Vatican Council, *Dogm. Const. on the Church, Lumen Gentium*, n. 10.

51. St Augustine, *Enarrat. in psalm.* 85:1: CCL 39, 1176.

52. Cf. Lk 10:21, when Jesus 'was filled with joy by the Holy Spirit and said, "I bless you, Father . . ." '.

53. Cf. Acts 2:42 (Greek text).

54. Cf. Mt 6:6.

55. Cf. Second Vatican Council, *Const. on Sacred Liturgy, Sacrosanctum Concilium*, n. 12.

56. Cf. *Ibid.*, n. 83–84.

57. Cf. *Ibid.*, n. 88.

58. Cf. *Ibid.*, n. 94.

59. Cf. Second Vatican Council, *Decree on Ministry and Life of Priests, Presbyterorum ordinis*, n. 5.

60. Second Vatican Council, *Decree of the Bishops' Pastoral Office in the Church, Christus Dominus*, n. 30.

61. Second Vatican Council, *Const. on Sacred Liturgy, Sacrosanctum Concilium*, n. 5.

62. Cf. *Ibid.*, nn. 83 & 98.

63. *Ibid.*, n. 7.

64. Cf. *Ibid.*, n. 10.

65. *Ibid.*, n. 33.

66. Cf. *Ibid.*, n. 24.

67. *Ibid.*, n. 33.

68. Cf. 1 Th 5:17.

69. Heb 23:15.

70. Second Vatican Council, *Const. on Sacred Liturgy, Sacrosanctum Concilium*, n. 84.

71. *Ibid.*, n. 85.

72. Cf. *Ibid.*, n. 83.

73. Second Vatican Council, *Dogm. Const. on the Church, Lumen gentium*, n. 50; cf. *Const. on Sacred Liturgy, Sacrosanctum Concilium*, nn. 8 & 104.

74. Second Vatican Council, *Dogm. Const. on the Church, Lumen gentium*, n. 48.

75. Cf. Rom 8:19.

76. Second Vatican Council, *Const. on Sacred Liturgy, Sacrosanctum Concilium*, n. 83.

77. Cf. Heb 5:7.

78. Cf. Second Vatican Council, *Decree on Ministry and Life of Priests, Presbyterorum ordinis*, n. 6.

79. Cf. Second Vatican Council, *Dogm. Const. on the Church, Lumen gentium*, n. 41.

80. Cf Below, n. 24.

81. Cf. Second Vatican Council, *Decree on Renewal of Religious Life, Perfectae caritatis*, n. 7.

82. Second Vatican Council, *Const. on Sacred Liturgy, Sacrosanctum Concilium*, n. 10.

83. *Ibid.*, n. 2.

84. Cf. John 15:5.

85. Cf. Second Vatican Council, *Const. on Sacred Liturgy, Sacrosanctum Concilium*, n. 86.

86. Cf. Eph 2:21–22.

87. Cf. Eph 4:13.

88. Cf. Second Vatican Council, *Const. on Sacred Liturgy, Sacrosanctum Concilium*, n. 2.

89. Cf. *Ibid.*, n. 90; St Benedict, *Regula Monasteriorum*, c. 19.

90. Cf. Second Vatican Council, *Decree on Ministry and Life of Priests, Presbyterorum ordinis*, n. 14; *Decree on Priestly Formation, Optatam Totius*, n. 8.

91. Cf. Second Vatican Council, *Const. on Sacred Liturgy, Sacrosanctum Concilium*, n. 26.

92. Cf. *Ibid.*, n. 41.

93. Second Vatican Council, *Decree on Bishops' Pastoral Office in the Church, Christus Dominus*, n. 11.

94. Second Vatican Council, *Const. on Sacred Liturgy, Sacrosanctum Concilium*, n. 42; cf. *Decree on Apostolate of the Laity, Apostolicam actuositatem*, n. 10.

95. Cf. Second Vatican Council, *Const. on Sacred Liturgy, Sacrosanctum Concilium*, nn. 26 & 84.

96. Cf. Second Vatican Council, *Decree on Church's Missionary Activity, Ad gentes*, n. 17.

97. Second Vatican Council, *Decree on the Bishop's Pastoral Office in the Church, Christus Dominus*, n. 15.

98. Cf. Second Vatican Council, *Const. on Sacred Liturgy, Sacrosanctum Concilium*, n. 100.

99. Cf. Second Vatican Council, *Decree on Ministry and Life of Priests, Presbyterorum ordinis*, n. 5.

100. Cf. Below, nn. 100–109.

101. Second Vatican Council, *Decree on the Bishops' Pastoral Office in the Church, Christus Dominus*, n. 33; cf. *Decree on Renewal of Religious Life, Perfectae caritatis*, nn. 6, 7, 15; *Decree on Church's Missionary Activity, Ad gentes*, n. 15.

102. Cf. Second Vatican Council, *Const. on Sacred Liturgy, Sacrosanctum Concilium*, n. 99.

103. Cf. *Ibid.*, n. 100.

104. Cf. John 4:23.

105. Cf. Second Vatican Council, *Declaration on Christian Education, Gravissimum educationis*, n. 2; *Decree on Apostolate of the Laity, Apostolicam actuositatem*, n. 16.

106. Cf. Second Vatican Council, *Decree on Apostolate of the Laity, Apostolicam actuositatem*, n. 11.

107. Cf. Second Vatican Council, *Decree on Ministry and Life of Priests, Presbyterorum ordinis*, n. 13.

108. Cf. Second Vatican Council, *Const. on Sacred Liturgy, Sacrosanctum Concilium*, n. 41; *Dogm. Const. on the Church, Lumen gentium*, n. 21.

109. Cf. Second Vatican Council, *Dogm. Const. on the Church, Lumen gentium*, n. 26; *Decree on the Bishops' Pastoral Office in the Church, Christus Dominus*, n. 15.

110. Cf. Second Vatican Council, *Decree on Ministry and Life of Priests, Presbyterorum ordinis*, n. 13.

111. Cf. *Ibid.*, n. 5.

112. Cf. John 10:11; 17:20, 23.

113. Cf. Second Vatican Council, *Const. on Sacred Liturgy, Sacrosanctum Concilium*, n. 90.

114. Cf. Second Vatican Council, *Dogm. Const. on the Church, Lumen gentium*, n. 41.

115. Cf. Second Vatican Council, *Dogm. Const. on Divine Revelation, Dei Verbum*, n. 25; *Decree on Ministry and Life of Priests, Presbyterorum ordinis*, n. 13.

116. Paul VI, Motu proprio, *Sacrum Diaconatus ordinem*, 18 June 1967, n. 27: *A.A.S.* 59 (1967), p. 703.

117. Cf. S. Congregation of Rites, Instruction *Inter Œcumenici*, 26 September 1964, n. 78 b: *A.A.S.* 56 (1964), p. 895.

118. Cf. Acts 4:32.

119. Cf. Second Vatican Council, *Const. on Sacred Liturgy, Sacrosanctum Concilium*, n. 100.

120. Cf. *Ibid.*, nn. 26, 28–30.

121. Cf. *Ibid.*, n. 27.

Chapter Two

1. Cf. Heb 3:7 – 4:16.

2. Second Vatican Council, *Const. on Sacred Liturgy, Sacrosanctum Concilium*, n. 89 a; cf. *Ibid.*, n. 100.

3. St Basil the Great, *Regulae fusius tractatae, Resp.* 37, 3: PG 31, 1014.

4. St Cyprian, *De oratione dominica*, 35: PL 4, 561.

5. St Basil the Great, *op. cit.*, PG 31, 1015.

6. Cf. Ps 140:2.

7. Cassian, *De institutione coenob.*, lib 3, c. 3: PL 49, 124, 125.

8. St Cyprian, *De oratione dominica*, 35: PL 4, 560.

9. *Pontificale Romanum, De ordinatione presbyterorum*, n. 14.

10. St Ambrose, *De officiis ministrorum* I, 20, 88: PL 16, 50. Second Vatican Council, *Dogm. Const. on Divine Revelation, Dei Verbum*, n. 25.

11. Second Vatican Council, *Const. on Sacred Liturgy, Sacrosanctum Concilium*, n. 89 c.

12. St. Augustine, *Sermo Guelferbytanus* 5:PLS 2:550.

13. *Ibid.*, PLS 2, 552.

14. Cf. Second Vatican Council, *Const. on Sacred Liturgy, Sacrosanctum Concilium*, n. 89 e.

15. Cf. *Ibid.*, n. 38.

Chapter Three

1. Second Vatican Council, *Const. on Sacred Liturgy, Sacrosanctum Concilium*, n. 90.

2. St Benedict, *Regula monasteriorum*, c. 19.

3. Cf. St Benedict, *ibid.*

4. Mt 22:44ff.

5. Cf. Second Vatican Council, *Const. on Sacred Liturgy, Sacrosanctum Concilium*, n. 91.

6. *Ibid.*, n. 102.

7. St Gregory the Great, *Homilia 34 in Evangelia:* PL 76, 1282.

8. Cf. Second Vatican Council, *Const. on Sacred Liturgy, Sacrosanctum Concilium*, n. 38.

9. St Vincent of Lirins, *Commonitorium*, 2: PL 50, 640.

10. St Bernard, *Sermo 3 in vigilia Nativitatis 1:* PL 183 (edit. 1879), 94.

11. Cf. Second Vatican Council, *Const. on Sacred Liturgy, Sacrosanctum Concilium*, n. 92 c.

12. Cf. *Ibid.*, n. 93.

13. Cf. *Ibid.*, n. 38.

14. For example, St John Chrysostom, *In Epist. ad Tim. I, Homilia* 6: PG 62, 530.

15. Cf. Second Vatican Council, *Const. on Sacred Liturgy, Sacrosanctum Concilium*, n. 38.

16. Cf. *Ibid.*, nn. 83 & 89.

17. Cf. below, n. 256.

18. Second Vatican Council, *Const. on Sacred Liturgy, Sacrosanctum Concilium*, n. 30.

Chapter Four

1. Cf. Second Vatican Council, *Const. on Sacred Liturgy, Sacrosanctum Concilium*, n. 100.

2. Cf. *Ibid.*, n. 111.

3. Cf. *Normae universales de anno liturgico et de calendario*, n. 52.

4. Cf. *Ibid.*, n. 52 c.

5. Cf. *Tabula dierum liturgicorum*, nn. 4 & 8.

6. Second Vatican Council, *Const. on Sacred Liturgy, Sacrosanctum Concilium*, n. 51.

7. Cf. Above, nn. 100–109.

Chapter Five

1. Second Vatican Council, *Const. on Sacred Liturgy, Sacrosanctum Concilium*, n. 28.

2. S. Congregation of Rites, Instruction *Musicam sacram*, 5 March 1967, n. 37: *A.A.S.* 59 (1967), p. 310; cf. Second Vatican Council, *Const. on Sacred Liturgy, Sacrosanctum Concilium*, n. 99.

3. Cf. Second Vatican Council, *Const. on Sacred Liturgy, Sacrosanctum Concilium*, n. 113.

4. Cf. *Ibid.*, n. 116.

5. S. Congregation of Rites, Instruction *Musicam sacram*, 5 March 1967, n. 9: *A.A.S.* 59 (1967), p. 303; cf. Second Vatican Council, *Const. on Sacred Liturgy, Sacrosanctum Concilium*, n. 116.

6. S. Congregation of Rites, Instruction *Musicam sacram*, 5 March 1967, n. 41; cf. nn. 54–61: *A.A.S.* 59 (1967), pp. 312, 316–317.

7. Cf. *Ibid.*, n. 51, p. 315.

8. Cf. *Ibid.*, n. 6: p. 302.

9. Cf. *Ibid.*, nn. 16a, 38: pp. 305, 311.

Part Two

Commentary on the Renewed Liturgy of the Hours

by A.-M. ROGUET, O.P.

Foreword

One of the most striking aspects of the liturgical renewal demanded by the Second Vatican Council has up to now remained completely unperceived by the public at large. This is because the communications media have failed to notice it: it is the *resurrection of the Liturgy of the Hours for the Christian people.*

Many of the faithful will wonder what this is and, when they know, they will be only moderately interested. All that had survived of the Liturgy of the Hours was Sunday Vespers (or, sometimes, Compline) and this attracted very few people to the churches, especially once Sunday evening Mass had become a regular feature. Why would anyone want to reanimate this corpse?

The answer, quite simply, is that the Divine Office is not a clerical or monastic preserve: it belongs to the Christian people. The Council expressed the desire that at least its principal Hours, namely Lauds and Vespers, should once again become popular (*Constitution on the Liturgy*, nn. 83, 87 and 100). Our churches today are used for scarcely anything apart from the celebration of Mass. While fully acknowledging the capital importance of the Mass, it is spiritually unhealthy that it should be separated from its traditional framework of prayer and praise. Certainly, the Mass already presents us with a most important element of divine praise and thanksgiving. However, one may reasonably ask whether Christians who never practise divine praise for its own sake, and who do not come to the church except when listening to the word of God and singing psalms are primarily a prelude to communion, have a true idea of what the Eucharist is. We normally associate the word Eucharist with the ideas of consecration, real presence and communion, but its primary meaning is adoration, praise, self-offering.

Certainly, our old Sunday Vespers seemed ill-suited to the demands and needs of the world. They were celebrated in Latin and mainly consisted of five psalms. The psalms were almost always the same, and they appeared somewhat exotic and archaic to Christians for whom the rest of the liturgy offered almost no contact with the Old Testament. The new Lectionary, however, has considerably 'opened up the treasures of the word of God'. The liturgical reform presents us with a Vespers (and Lauds) which can be celebrated in the vernacular; the psalms are more varied and fewer in number; the biblical reading and homily, the Prayers of intercession, and the Our Father, solemnly sung by all, should make these Hours more interesting, more relevant, and more popular.

The Council desired that the Liturgy of the Hours should be revived in our Christian communities. Will this in fact happen?[1]

In a modest way, this Commentary hopes to help achieve that end, by expounding the content and meaning of the renewed Liturgy of the Hours, in three chapters, as follows:

I. Theology: What is the basis, meaning, and significance of this form of prayer?

II. Liturgy: What of the structure and individual parts of this renewed prayer of praise? We shall present this as it is, without going into the history of the Divine Office, since this is unlikely to be of general interest. We shall not devote much space to rubrical details.

III. Spirituality: The reader who has persevered to this chapter will realize that the renewal of the Liturgy of the Hours among the faithful does offer an opportunity to practise a prayer of praise. Without it the liturgical renewal runs the risk of falling short of the mark.

It is certainly excellent to make the liturgy more accessible so that all may participate, to translate it into the vernacular, and to link it with people's daily life. But it still needs to achieve completely 'that great work of giving perfect praise to God and making men holy' (*Constitution on the Liturgy*, n. 7).

If the work of glorifying God is forgotten, or is relegated to a second place, we shall no longer be dealing with genuine liturgy but with a 'horizontal' and insipid kind of humanism.

The first of all the commandments, Jesus tells us, is this:

'Listen, Israel,
the Lord our God is the one Lord,
and you must love the Lord your God

1. At Notre Dame Cathedral in Paris, a large and prayerful congregation gathers each Sunday for Lauds and Vespers, and on feast days the Cathedral is full at these hours.

with all your heart, with all your soul,
with all your mind and with all your strength' (Mark 12:28–30).

This is the commandment that the Liturgy of the Hours helps us to accomplish.

Bibliographical Note

The whole of this work is a commentary on the principles of the renewal of the Liturgy of the Hours as established by Vatican II's *Constitution on the Liturgy*. We refer to this document by the abbreviation CL and the number of the article.

In particular, however, we shall be commenting on the *General Instruction on the Liturgy of the Hours*, issued by the Sacred Congregation for Divine Worship, which forms Part One of this present volume, and is to be printed at the beginning of the volumes containing the Liturgy of the Hours. We refer to this document by the abbreviations LH and the number of the article.

Those who wish to become better acquainted with the history of the Divine Office, may consult P. Salmon, *L'office divin*, Paris, 1969; or the same author's brief exposition, 'La prière des heures', in A. G. Martimort, *L'Eglise en prière*, Paris-Rome, 1965, pp. 809–902.

In the actual practice of the Liturgy of the Hours, and particularly on celebration in common, see the symposium, *Célébrer l'office divin*, coll. Kinnor, Paris, 1967.

Chapter One

Theology

What is the Liturgy of the Hours? What is its nature, its meaning, its usefulness? This first chapter attempts a reply to this fundamental question.

While studies on the theology of the Mass abound, little has been written on the Divine Office.

But as its name implies, the Liturgy of the Hours forms a part of the liturgy as a whole. We can therefore apply to it the fundamental principles of the liturgy, such as were expounded with especial authority in the *Constitution on the Liturgy*.[1] We should remember too that the whole of the liturgy 'has its heart and centre in the Eucharistic mystery'[2]: the Eastern Church calls 'the liturgy' what we call 'the Mass'.

This presentation of the theology of the Liturgy of the Hours will follow a very simple pattern. We shall first of all recall those elements of the theology of the Mass which are *common* both to the Mass and to the Liturgy of the Hours. We shall then consider those elements which are *proper* to the Liturgy of the Hours and which therefore distinguish it from the Mass. We shall use for this the relatively new considerations which are offered us by the *General Instruction on the Liturgy of the Hours*.

By way of concluding this parallel between the Liturgy of the Hours and the Mass, we shall try to answer the question: can the Liturgy of the Hours be considered as a sacrifice?

I. Characteristics Common to the Mass and to the Liturgy of the Hours

1. A Prayer of Praise and Thanksgiving

Praise is the primary duty of a Christian towards God, and indeed of any creature towards the creator. As St Ignatius of Loyola says forcefully in the 'Foundations' of the *Spiritual*

1. Above all in the foreword and the first chapter, particularly articles 1 to 14.
2. Paul VI, the Encyclical *Mysterium fidei*.

Exercises: 'Man was created to praise, venerate and serve the Lord his God, and in that way to save his soul.'

But what is *praise*? Like all basic realities and attitudes – life, death, love – it is very difficult to define. It is essentially an unlimited appreciation of the grandeur of God, a loving appreciation which expresses itself in words, and better still in song. It is not a cold and objective statement, but warm and human acknowledgement of God. God is not merely a truth to be known. 'He alone is good'[3] and moves us to love him. He is also the fulness of beauty, and has a right to our total admiration.[4]

Vocal praise which we find in the liturgy is like the sacrament or visible sign of adoration – even though adoration expresses itself more profoundly in silence. As creatures of flesh and blood, we naturally want to express this adoration.

Thanksgiving can, at first sight, appear less sublime and less self-interested than praise. While praise considers God in himself, thanksgiving considers him in relation to us. But really, it is impossible to consider God in himself. He is always *God for us.* Thanksgiving is in fact just as absolute and all-embracing as praise. We thank God for all that he has given us: not only for everything that we have, but for what we are. We thank him for all that exists, and therefore for himself above all. Thanksgiving cannot be reduced to a *quid pro quo*, for what God has given us, as if we were merely paying off a debt. Thanksgiving is the acknowledgement of an infinite debt that we could never pay. That is why 'thanksgiving' has become an irreplaceable quality of Christianity.

3. Mk 10:18 and parallel Synoptic texts.

4. Theology and spirituality, at least in the West (see on the contrary Denys, *Divine Names*, ch. IV), hardly speak of the beauty of God at all. This is probably due in part to the fact that all our translations, beginning with the Vulgate, translate by *bonus*, good, the biblical terms *tôb* and *kalos*, which mean *beautiful* as well as good. It is thus that we call 'the good shepherd' the *kalos poimèn* of John 10. The theme of 'glory' is obviously very close to that of beauty, and its link with praise is very close (cf. Ep 1:6.12.14). A biblical study of the beauty of God would lead us immediately to Ps 95:6, and to the nuptial theme of the beauty of the spouse (Ps 44; Song of Songs, *passim*). For the beauty of Christ, cf. Hebrews 1:3 and the Transfiguration. We should also notice this phrase in CL art. 122: 'Very rightly the fine arts are considered to rank among the noblest expressions of human genius. This judgement applies especially to religious art and to its highest achievement, which is sacred art. By their nature both of the latter are related to *God's boundless beauty*, for this is the reality which these human efforts are trying to express in some way . . . they are dedicated to God and to the cause of his *greater honour and glory*' (Our italics).

It brings to mind another mystery. The Greek *Eucharistia* comes from *charis* which means grace, the gratuitous gift of God. God pours out his grace upon us, without any merit on our part. He first loved us (1 John 5:5). Our thanksgiving is a response to his love. It is an echo of his goodness to us: thanksgiving, like praise, is a supernatural act which has its origin and its full expression in the gift of God. As one of the new prefaces of the Roman Missal is entitled: praise, the gift of God.[5]

It is hardly necessary to point out that the Mass is a sacrifice of thanksgiving, since that is its true name: Eucharist. The term comes from the Institution narrative: 'Jesus . . . took bread . . . gave you thanks (*eucharistèsas*), . . . gave it to his disciples, and said: ". . . this is my body . . . given up for you".'[6]

Thanksgiving is unceasingly expressed in the Mass, above all in the preface which opens the prayer of consecration and gives the whole prayer a quality of thanksgiving.

That the Liturgy of the Hours is essentially a prayer of praise and thanksgiving is easily seen from the fact that it principally consists of psalms, which are by definition hymns of thanksgiving and praise, even if in many of them lamentation seems to be the dominating theme. Lamentation often has an important role in psalms which were specifically written as psalms of thanksgiving: by drawing attention to his distress the psalmist magnifies the power and mercy of God's deliverance.[7] In many psalms we find the psalmist beset with trials, yet trusting in God's deliverance and promising to give thanks when God has heard him.[8]

There is thus a harmony between the Liturgy of the Hours

5. Common Preface IV, *De laude, dono Dei.* This is an English translation:
. . . All-powerful and eternal God.
You do not need our praise,
yet it is you
who moves us to give you thanks:
our songs add nothing to what you are,
but they draw us near to you
through Christ our Lord.

6. Words of the first eucharistic prayer (the Roman Canon), which are close to the words of the institution narratives given in the New Testament. For the bread Lk 22:19 and I Cor 11:24 have 'to give thanks', while Mt 26:26 and Mk 14:22 have 'to bless'. But these words are synonomous (it is God who is blessed), and moreover Mt and Mk use the word 'to give thanks' shortly afterwards for the words over the cup.

7. Cf. Ps 21:26–32; 29; 34:28; 39:4; 55:11; 65:15–17 and above all 114–115.

8. Cf. Ps 7:18; 12:6; 56:8–9; 68:31–35; 78:13; 85:12; 101:22–23.

and the Mass: it both prepares for the Mass and continues it. Our devotion for the Mass should inspire in us a devotion for the Liturgy of the Hours. Why is this not in fact the case? Because too many Christians look on the Mass as a mystery of the descent of God amongst us, and consider the Liturgy of the Hours as the ascent of our prayers towards God. In this perspective, the Mass seems important for our salvation, while the Liturgy of the Hours appears as a profusion of words without any particular effect, a leisure activity for the devout. This apparent opposition between the two ceases if we see them as they really are: the ascent of our hearts and gifts to God who, as our creator and saviour, has the right to demand our thanksgiving.

2. A Community Prayer in Christ

We can obviously thank and praise God in prayer, but the duty to praise God cannot be restricted to individuals or to the silence of private prayer: it is a duty of the Church as such, and normally finds its expression in word and song. Moreover, we are dealing with *liturgy*. Etymologically, this word calls to mind a sacred action carried out on behalf of the people (*laos*) of God.

Neither the Mass nor the Liturgy of the Hours are the prayers of individual faithful, nor of people who happen to have come together by chance. They are the prayers of a community, precisely as a community. Yet this does not sufficiently state their nature, since there are many devotions carried out in common, such as the recitation of rosary, which are not 'sacred actions'. They do not belong to the liturgy as such.[9]

We can only speak of liturgy when the community acts in so far as it is the Church, and because the Church herself recognizes it under the movement of the Holy Spirit who is her soul and conscience: this is the case both with the Liturgy of the Hours and with the Mass.

When there is a truly liturgical action, the community which performs it represents the Church, it *is* the Church. However small and poor a community may be, when it celebrates the liturgy it is a particular Church. This is above all true of the local churches, the parishes. But it is also true of personal parishes, of little groups which celebrate the liturgy, and therefore of religious communities. By reason of their homo-

9. Cf. CL 13.

geneous nature, these communities are less representative of the universal Church than is a mixed congregation of different sexes, social classes, cultural backgrounds and religious fervour. For this reason it is always a good thing that a religious community should join in the celebration of the Mass and the Office with the faithful at large.

Whenever it celebrates the liturgy, each local church causes the universal Church to be present. When a small community celebrates the Liturgy of the Hours, it renders to God the duties of the whole Church.[10]

The Church is Christ. 'It is all one,' said Joan of Arc. In the words of Bossuet: 'The Church is Jesus Christ, but Jesus Christ as poured out and communicated to man.' In the liturgy, Christ exercises through the whole Church, head and members (Christ and all the baptized) his priestly work of glorifying the Father, and of saving and sanctifying the whole human race.[11]

When the Church celebrates the liturgy, Christ is really present.

This is a doctrine, which, already outlined in Pius XII's encyclical on the liturgy *Mediator Dei*, has been expounded with greater precision in the *Constitution on the Liturgy* (7), and in the 1967 Instruction *Eucharisticum Mysterium* (art. 9). In his encyclical *Mysterium Fidei* Pope Paul VI once again took up and developed this theme.

We must remember that this presence of Christ in the liturgy is a *real presence*. Catholics normally reserve the use of this phrase to the presence of Christ under the eucharistic species, but it may also be used of those modes of presence that we are about to enumerate. The phrase real presence means that we are not dealing with a conceptual or purely spiritual presence, which would depend on the merits, attention, or state of grace of the individual, and which would therefore vary according to those taking part. We are speaking of an effective, actual presence, which depends on objective conditions that are easily verifiable.

In a series of progressive steps which correspond to the unfolding of the celebration, we can point to a real presence of

10. On the sacramentality (in political language one would say: representativity) of small liturgical assemblies with regard to the universal Church, cf. CL 26, 42; *Lumen Gentium*, 26, 28; but above all the Instruction *Eucharisticum mysterium* of 25 May 1967, 18, 26–27.

11. Cf. CL 7.

Christ in his Church and in the Church's liturgy in four ways.[12]

1) By the very fact that the Church is gathered together, that she prays and sings the psalms, Christ is present in accordance with his promise: 'When two or three are gathered together in my name, there am I in the midst of them' (Matthew 18:20). When the Church prays and sings, Christ prays and sings with her and in her.

2) When the word of God is proclaimed, Christ is present: even when the Old Testament is read it is he who speaks, according to all the Fathers, since he is the eternal Word and divine Wisdom.

3) By reason of the fact that a priest consecrates the bread and wine in the assembly, Christ is present in this priest who affirms: 'This is my body . . .', and it is the body of Christ which becomes present.

4) This consecration makes Christ present in the species of bread and wine in a real way, but also in a substantial (that is to say that Christ entirely takes the place of the whole bread, except for the appearances), personal (that is to say that it is not the action or influence of Christ merely, but the very person of Christ, God and man) and permanent way.

This last characteristic of the presence of Christ is proper to the eucharistic species alone, and explains why they should be adored – which is not the case for the other forms of presence: we do not adore either the word of God, or the priest! These first three modes of presence are dynamic and transitory: they cease with the celebration and, as far as the priest is concerned, once the consecration is over.

If the last two modes of presence are characteristic of the eucharistic celebration, the first two are common to all liturgical actions. We find them in the first part of the Mass, leaving aside for the moment their fulfilment in the Eucharist; in sacred celebrations of the word of God without the Eucharist, for example in a marriage or funeral without the celebration of Mass; and, finally, in the celebration of the Office. So the Office, like the Mass, and like all liturgical actions, is an act of the whole Church and of Christ present in her.

12. *The Constitution on the Liturgy* also mentions a presence of Christ 'by his power in the sacraments'; in his Encyclical *Mysterium fidei* Pope Paul VI also mentions the presence of Christ in the poor, but here we are moving beyond the liturgy. By reason of our purpose we limit ourselves to the four modes of presence as given in the Instruction *Eucharisticum mysterium*, and in the same order.

Christ, therefore, is really present when the Liturgy of the Hours is celebrated, especially when the psalms are being sung or the word of God is being read. We shall have reason to return to this point when we examine the role of the psalms and of the readings of the word of God in the Hours.

We may find it difficult to recognize the intimate relationship between the Mass and the Office. Every Christian, however little the liturgical movement has affected him, will readily admit that the Mass is not an act of private devotion but a community celebration. This is not so clear in the case of the Liturgy of the Hours. Often enough, we think of a priest reciting *his* breviary on his own. There is a misunderstanding of the nature of the Office in this, against which the reform we are now trying to present is a vigorous reaction.

By its nature, the Liturgy of the Hours is a solemn and communal celebration. That is what it was in its origins. As the work of the clergy became more extensive and more demanding, and their way of life became more and more individualistic, the Office was celebrated more often than not in private. The Church however, has always considered this as something to be tolerated, as a concession. It has never admitted the principle of private celebration as normal, and still less as the ideal. By reciting his Office privately the priest is making up for the fact that he is not able to celebrate it in common. Private celebration remains linked to celebration in common – even by the retention of formulas such as *Dominus Vobiscum*, which are scarcely adapted to private celebration and presuppose that more than one person is present.

This development of the liturgy of the Hours towards individual celebration has been encouraged by an individualistic and juridical notion of obligation, linked to the personal quality of clergy in sacred orders.[13] It has brought with it the serious disadvantage of *clericalizing* the Liturgy of the Hours. The Office has come to be considered as the professional preserve of the clergy, and for the laity it seemed to be a luxury reserved to an élite or to eccentrics enjoying considerable leisure. One of the most noteworthy features in the ecclesiology of the Second Vatican Council, especially in its dogmatic Constitution on the Church, *Lumen Gentium*, is that the Church is

13. A well documented study of this development may be found in Chapter I of P. Salmon, *L'Office divin* (*Lex Orandi* 27), Paris 1959.

not merely envisaged as a hierarchal society – which it evidently is – but above all as a communion, a communion of the people of God, of all the baptized.

This is the fundamental reason, the dogmatic reason, why the liturgical reform recommends that the Liturgy of the Hours should be celebrated solemnly and in a community, using song as far as possible, and encouraging the participation of the laity. This participation of the laity should not be considered as a devotion merely added on to the celebration accomplished by the clergy: the laity, the Christian people, should consider this prayer as *their* prayer. (We expand this point later, cf. no. 7)

The Liturgy of the Hours, then, like the Mass itself, is a celebration belonging to the whole Church – by which we mean here all those who, by reason of their baptism, share in the priesthood of Christ.

3 A Prayer which has a Role in the Economy of Salvation

Christ, and the Church in which he is present, are those who act in the liturgy. But they are living beings, their action is within the context of the world's history. In the unfolding of God's plan for mankind, their role is seen and achieved in the economy of salvation. Christianity is not a school of philosophy entrusted with revealing and maintaining eternal, abstract and static truths. It is a history: that is one of the most important themes of the Second Vatican Council. Revelation itself takes place in and through history, in so far as God speaks through events. In a reciprocal way, his word properly so-called, the prophecies, the teachings of Jesus, the writings of the New Testament, all have the purpose of giving us an understanding of this history.[14] His acts are words, just as his word throws light on his acts.

Consequently, when the Church, with Christ present in her, celebrates the liturgy, she is not merely calling to mind and celebrating the same mystery day after day, or just repeating the same prayer. By this celebration which is rooted in and based upon a memorial (which does not throw us back into the past, but which makes this past present *today*), the Church

14. We merely note the definition of revelation given in *The Constitution on Revelation, Dei Verbum*, art. 2.

lives, grows, discovers, and becomes aware of her present situation while moving forward to her future.

That is what is meant by the fact, which routine prevents us from noticing, that the Mass and the Office follow the course of the Church's year. They pass through a long cycle of seasons and feasts which are not repeated in the course of the same year, and which are not interchangeable. Only a very inattentive observer would think this series of Masses and Hours constitutes a boring repetition, a series of identical and perpetually repeated prayers. These liturgical actions are a part of the history of the Church: they bring about a deeper and deeper penetration of human history by the mystery of Christ. Christ is not just a figure from the past, the historical founder of the Church and the person who instituted the sacraments; nor is it sufficient to say that he is with us, accompanying us and sustaining us on our journey: he stands at the end of our journey; he calls us and draws us to him, he is our hope and our future.[15]

Later (no 6) we shall see that the Office is even more intimately related to time than it is to the Mass, since each of its parts is affected by a particular time of the day: an 'Hour'.

4. An Eschatological Prayer, A Foretaste of Heaven

The life of the Church and her prayer look towards, wait for and even hasten (2 Peter 3:12) towards their final consummation. Christ is the author and the principal actor of this prayer. It is Christ, already glorious in heaven where he has prepared a place for us (John 14:2), who is there in his humanity, with Mary and with the angels. Mary is a symbol of the Church, and by the mystery of her assumption she too is in heaven, while the other saints who are there still await the glorification of their bodies.

By making us praise God in union with heaven, both the Mass and the Office have an eschatological quality. This is clearly expressed in the final verses of all the Prefaces at Mass which introduce the hymn of the Seraphim (Isaiah 6:1–3), the *Sanctus*. The same is true of those other parts of the eucharistic prayer in which we invoke the saints.

15. This is one of the great Pauline themes: see for example 2 Cor 4:13 – 5:10, and above all Ph 3.

There is a spiritual tradition which has always seen in the celebration of praise at the Liturgy of the Hours a truly angelic function, and it explains why the monastic life is often called an 'angelic life'. Whether they are monks, priests, or lay people, all those who take part in the Liturgy of the Hours are not only sanctifying their earthly life, and finding strength and consolation in the Office: they are anticipating the life of heaven and already savouring a foretaste of eternal life.[16]

5. Praise and Intercession

But we are not yet in heaven!

We are still on earth, and the Church shares in the struggles and vicissitudes of men on earth. She is involved. Her liturgy should not be an alibi, a pretext for escapism.

Even in its purely theocentric aspect, namely in its praise and thanksgiving, the Church remains in the world, she prays with men as they suffer and as they struggle, and she prays for them. To celebrate the glory of God is not to escape from the world. Praise is a duty for God's creatures, and by performing this duty the Church works for the salvation of the world. The entire liturgy thus has a double function: a theocentric one, of praise, and an anthropocentric one. At one and the same time she glorifies God and achieves the salvation of man, just as Christ offered himself on the cross both to glorify his Father and to save mankind. To separate these two functions is to destroy the liturgy. A liturgy of pure praise would not really be human. It could be an aesthetic experience, but it would be without apostolic value; it would be indifferent to the needs and misery of men. A liturgy of intercession alone, however, would merely present us with man and his self-interest, forgetting the primacy of the glory of God.[17]

The Mass is indeed a Eucharist. It is a full acknowledgement of God's glory, but it is none the less a prayer for the Church and for man. This anthropocentric side of the liturgy is particularly in evidence in the penitential preparation, the *Kyrie* and the prayers; in those parts of intercession where the eucharistic prayer is an intercession for the Church, for the living and the dead; in the second part of the Our Father and in the prayers

16. Cf. CL 8 for the liturgy in general; for the divine office cf. CL 83, LH 15–16.

17. This reference to the two inextricably linked purposes of the liturgy recurs constantly in CL: 2, 5, 6, 7, 10, 33, etc.

for peace. The restoration of the Prayer of the Faithful to the Mass has even further emphasized the prayer of Christians at the Eucharist for all the needs of their brothers.

The Liturgy of the Hours would not be a true liturgy if it were nothing else but praise. Its anthropocentric character is found in those many psalms which pray God to have mercy on human misery, psalms which are said in the name of all sinners, of all in need, of all men. It must be admitted that the Office sometimes seemed too far removed from human realities. This undoubtedly explains people's preference for Compline. In comparison with the theocentric emphasis of Vespers, Compline seemed more human and more digestible.

Any reform of the Office which intended to make this prayer more attractive and accessible to the Christian people has to emphasize this concern for the needs of our brothers. Following monastic tradition then, it has once again found a place in the Office for the recitation (or even better, the singing) of the Our Father. More especially, it has restored the prayers of intercession. On certain days of the year these prayers had always remained in the Office, but in a very dessicated form. They have now been restored not only as in the prayers of the faithful, at each Sunday Mass, but twice each day in the morning and in the evening (see no 15 below).

On this last point, one would hope that the deep love for the Mass among priests and laity might extend to this Liturgy of the Hours. Like the Mass, and even more so in a way, it allows us to intercede for all the needs of the world.

II. Special Characteristics of the Liturgy of the Hours

6. The Consecration of Time

The subject of our book is generally referred to at the present time as the breviary. This word is misleading. Firstly, because it suggests a book and not a liturgical action: we never say that a priest is celebrating the Missal. At one time it must have been equally strange to say that he recites the breviary. Secondly, the word breviary was used to describe an abbreviated book. It was a book which was easy to handle. It allowed clergy who were obliged to travel, or who were unable to take part in the solemn celebration of the Hours, to recite them in private without having to use the entire liturgical library needed for community celebration. Finally, the breviary had become the vade-mecum of the clergy. It would have been almost as strange to see it in the hands of a layman as to see him wearing a biretta!

A far better expression is 'the Divine Office'. This is the term used by *Mediator Dei* and by the *Constitution on the Liturgy*. It means that the praise of God is a duty to be carried out. Yet, at the same time, this is too general a term, since it applied equally well to the Mass. It encompassed, in fact, both the Mass and the Liturgy of the Hours. They constituted the daily obligation for chapters and monasteries.

The Constitution on the Liturgy indicates that what is called the Divine Office is 'by tradition going back to early Christian times, arranged so that the whole course of the day and night is made holy by the praises of God' (art. 84). '*The purpose of the Office is to sanctify the day*,' and that is why the traditional sequence (*cursus*, the cycle) of the Hours was to be restored so that as far as possible they might be once again *genuinely related to the time of the day* at which they are prayed. 'Moreover, it will be necessary to take into account the modern conditions in which daily life has to be lived, especially by those who are called on to labour in apostolic works' (art. 88). Therefore, the principal purpose of the Liturgy of the Hours is the sanctification of time through the recitation of the Hours according to the different times of the day. That is why what has up to now been called the breviary or the Divine Office is better described by the phrase *the Liturgy of the Hours*. We use this name very frequently here, as does the official document on which we are commenting, *The General Instruction on the Liturgy of the Hours*. That document does not even use the term breviary when it is describing the book containing the Office: it refers to 'the book of the Liturgy of the Hours'.

The name now adopted is more precise than 'Divine Office', since it excludes the Mass. The celebration of Mass has a very important part to play in the consecration of time, since many of its expressions reflect the cycle of the liturgical year; the words of the Mass, however, are not related to any particular *hour* of the day. The 1917 code of canon law contained many canons regulating the time of day when Mass could be celebrated (can. 821, par. 1; 867, par. 4), but these rules were reasonably flexible; they allowed for many exceptions in indult; since the introduction of evening Mass and the easing of the eucharistic fast, these canons have almost entirely lost their original force.

What is more, even as regards the sanctification of the day itself, there is a remarkable fact which is unknown to many of the faithful: in Christian antiquity in the West the celebration of Mass was not everywhere a daily occurrence. There were 'a-liturgical' days, and there still are such days in the East. Yet in the East as in the West, daily celebration of the Hours is the norm. As far as the individual priest is concerned, Roman legislation has for several centuries made it a grave obligation to recite the entire Office each day, but it has not imposed a similar obligation regarding the daily celebration of Mass.

Let us come back to the Liturgy of the Hours. They have the purpose of sanctifying time – but not time in general, nor even the day taken as a block. As we have seen, *The Constitution on the Liturgy* speaks of 'the traditional sequence of the Hours'. It is a tradition which present usage has almost completely obscured. The code of canon law says: 'Clerics in major orders (namely subdeacons, deacons, priests and bishops) are obliged to recite all the canonical Hours each day . . .' (Can. 135). The 'Hours', while still retaining their name in this text, are put forward as forming a complete whole, an obligatory dose of daily prayer. Given this view, a person might be scrupulous about omitting even the least part, but not be in the least concerned about saying them all one after another. The concern of most priests was not so much to say them at the right time of day, but to have said them all before midnight (or one o'clock, in countries where the hour was one hour ahead . . .). In this way that 'genuine relation to the time of the day', so strongly emphasized by the Council, went largely unheeded. This meant that one was rising with the dawn at ten o'clock at night, and asking for a night without bad dreams at two o'clock in the afternoon! A prayer which continually uses formulas which are completely unrealistic is not only in conflict with objective truth: psychologically, it cannot be taken seriously. It becomes an empty formality that is carried out because it is obligatory, but without a person really being able to give it full-hearted attention. It is undoubtedly meritorious by virtue of obedience and of the general intention to carry out a good work, but it cannot be said for its own sake, and less still is it able to arouse the enthusiasm indispensable for saying it well.

Under the influence of the liturgical renewal many priests had already made it their rule to recite each hour at the correct time. While it was often very difficult to organize the day in that way, it did allow them to recover a taste for the Office. It was no longer a burdensome task best dealt with in long stretches at a time, with some priests prudently reciting it as soon as possible while others, resigned and weary, recited it all at the end of the day. For those who wanted to maintain that 'genuine relationship to the time of the day', the Office marked the various stages of the day, sanctifying it from the beginning to the end, not overburdening the attention with an unending series of psalms . . . For those priests, who, without being activists, were engaged in the ministry, this recitation 'at the right time' was extremely difficult to achieve since their daily activity did not allow a steady and unchanging rhythm. The regular pattern of the Office reflects its monastic origins. In a rural style of life where the pattern of activity is regulated according to position of the sun, it was possible to recite the Hours at 'the right Hour' – retiring at the same time as the animals of the fields, rising in the middle of the night, and making a very early start to the day. In urban life where the evening has assumed far greater importance, people scarcely knew where to place the large block which made up Matins. The morning hours became terribly crowded if you wanted to fit in Lauds, Prime and Terce, besides meditation and the daily celebration of Mass . . .

It is necessary to pray always, to pray without ceasing (Luke 18:1; 1 Thessalonians 5:17), or at least to move in that direction by breaking up the day with frequent prayers. The purpose of the Hours was to try and achieve this continuity, and in earlier days it had seemed to the monks that by multiplying the Hours you came closer to the angelic ideal. In point of fact, the Office cannot provide us with a continual liturgical prayer. Human life always has its dead or at least indifferent moments: sleep, washing and dressing, house-work, cooking, eating . . . life also demands activities from which the liturgical life cannot exclude us: work, study, apostolate, human relationships, cultural and leisure activities. The Hours can never be other than high-points, somewhat like, if you permit the comparison, the *Hour* of Jesus, which according to Saint John is a crucial moment since it gives a certain significance to his whole life.

We were left with the paradoxical result that the multiplication of the Hours ended by emptying them of their meaning, leaving them burdensome and tedious by separating them, almost necessarily, from the time at which they were meant to be said.

The purpose of the liturgical reform in cutting down the number of Hours in reducing the number of psalms and readings, has not been to minimize the importance of prayer. To assert the contrary would be to identify the number of words with the spiritual quality of the prayer. By reducing their number and their length, the value of the Hours has been reasserted. They can recover their original meaning by being able to be said at the right time of the day and without demanding a tremendous effort of will power to do so.

An Office designed for monks is not suited for use by the laity. For the laity there were 'little Offices' which were simpler and shorter than the 'big Office'. Certain religious congregations, even cloistered congregations like the Sisters of the Visitation, used what is best described as a *digest* or an *ersatz*. Besides being relatively monotonous and threadbare, these Offices, though approved by the Church, were not properly speaking the prayer of the Church.

The Constitution on the Liturgy admits these little Offices. Under certain conditions, and this is new, she even considers them as truly 'liturgical'. Nevertheless, it is desirable, and undoubtedly this is what will happen, that the active congregations and the laity should prefer to say the Liturgy of the Hours, now that it has been made more accessible. Even if not all the Hours are said each day, one will be carrying out a genuinely liturgical function, knowing that one prays with the Church and in union with all her members.

7. 'Praise . . . Belongs to the Entire Christian Community'

It is certain that the Mass, like the rest of the liturgy, 'belongs to the whole Christian community'. However, as every Catholic knows, Mass cannot be celebrated if there is no ministerial priest presiding over the people – who are themselves endowed with the priesthood common to all the baptized. Only the ministerial priest has received through his ordination by a bishop, the successor and heir of the apostles, the power to act personally in the place of Christ for the consecrating and offering of the sacrifice of his body and blood. Without the priest, the Christian people cannot offer the eucharistic sacrifice.

On the other hand, while it is good that a sacred minister – bishop, priest or deacon – should preside over the Liturgy of the Hours, he is not indispensable. Whether it be a group of lay-brothers or nuns, a group of lay people, or even a lay person on his own – if they celebrate the Liturgy of the Hours, they are truly praying the prayer of the Church, with Christ, and their celebration is 'liturgical' in the fullest sense of the word.

The reader, perhaps, will find this statement quite obvious: it follows quite naturally from the priesthood common to all the baptized, and the Christians of the early centuries would have had no doubts on the subject.

It should however, be pointed out that this doctrine constitutes a reversal of, or if you prefer, a reaction against the liturgical-canonical position of the Church in the last century. It was held that the Liturgy of the Hours could not be accomplished liturgically, as a priestly act of the Church, except by persons *deputed* for this task, namely clerics in sacred orders, monks and nuns. In 1947, the encyclical *Mediator Dei* stated it as self-evident: in order to represent the Church in official prayer you must 'be delegated for this purpose'.

The Constitution on the Liturgy of 1963 reflects a development. It begins by saying (art. 84) that the Office is liturgical when it is 'rendered by priests and others who are *deputed for this purpose by Church ordinance*, or by the faithful praying together with the priest in an approved form'.

On reading this text, one might have thought that the Divine Office sung regularly by a congregation with simple vows was not a liturgical act, while the breviary muttered by a priest in his bedroom or in the tube or subway was recognized as being liturgical. The text of the *Constitution* enlarged these juridical conditions by recognizing (art. 98) the liturgical value of the Office, when recited even in part by 'the members of any institute dedicated to acquiring perfection'. The laity too were encouraged to recite the Divine Office among themselves, and even individually (art. 100), but it was not said that their celebration of the Office would thereby be liturgical.

The General Instruction on the Liturgy of the Hours goes much further. It certainly recognizes that since their profession dedicates them to prayer, priests and religious have a 'special mandate' – but not an exclusive one – as regards the Liturgy of the Hours (n. 17). It is for them to announce and to direct the prayer of the community of the faithful (n. 23). *All* religious or members of a secular institute 'have a particular relationship with the Liturgy of the Hours, since their spiritual life consecrates them to the good of the whole Church' (n. 24). The laity are invited '*to carry out the duty of the Church* by celebrating a part of the Liturgy of the Hours' (n. 27).

Clergy in major orders, however, have a further obligation to celebrate this liturgy. The Church 'deputes' them, not just as something individual and juridical, but in the interest both of this prayer and of the Christian people, in order that 'the *duty of the whole community* may be constantly and continuously fulfilled and the prayer of Christ may persevere unceasingly in the Church.' (n. 28).

Finally, in n. 270, we find this statement given in passing, and therefore as if self-evident: 'By reason of its origin and of its character, the praise of the Church should not be reserved to monks and clerics: it belongs to the whole Christian community.'

This liberation from the excessively individualistic juridicism of past generations is not just in the realm of theory. It should help draw both lay people and pastors to the celebration of divine praise.

The laity who recite the Liturgy of the Hours are not particularly outstanding Christians like Pascal or Paul Claudel; nor are they eccentrics pretending to be monks or ecclesiastics. When carrying out the duty of the priestly people, they do not cease to be laity, consecrated by baptism to divine worship.

As far as pastors are concerned, they should no longer see the Liturgy of the Hours – as perhaps they did – as a clerical occupation (not to say burden), or as a relic of monasticism, which separated them from their people. They celebrate the Liturgy of the Hours for their people, but also with their people. They too are baptized! Most of them, without forgetting their ministerial priesthood, are well aware that the Mass they celebrate even in private, is not *their* Mass but the sacrifice of the whole Christian people offered through their hands. It will be even easier for them to see that in the celebration the Liturgy of the Hours they are not separated from the Christian people. On the contrary, they are more deeply identified with their people.

III. Can the Liturgy of the Hours be Considered as a Sacrifice?

We have attempted to outline a theology of the Liturgy of the Hours by comparing it with the Mass. The Mass is above all defined as a sacrifice: is there also a certain sacrificial character in the Liturgy of the Hours?

At first sight it seems not. In the Mass there are external realities, things we can see: bread and wine. The priest consecrates them and, through this consecration, they become the body and blood of Jesus, immolated and offered up for the glory of God and the salvation of mankind. We do not find anything of this kind in the Liturgy of the Hours: there is no consecration, there is nothing like bread and wine that we can feel and see; there is no communion in consecrated gifts. In the Mass, we are doing or 'making' something. According to the etymology of the word sacrifice we are 'making something sacred'. In the Liturgy of the Hours, we do not 'make' anything: we speak, we sing and we listen.

One might well ask whether this radical contrast does not underlie the attitude of many Christians who, although they have a deep love for the Mass, have no interest at all in the Liturgy of the Hours. At Mass, they feel, we offer the sacrifice of Christ, we go to communion and we receive God's graces, while in the Liturgy of the Hours nothing happens. If it does not *do* anything, it has no use: it is a waste of time.

In the Liturgy of the Hours we can in fact discern a certain sacrificial character, by analogy to the sacrifice which Catholic doctrine attributes to the Mass.

We should not consider sacrifice merely from a material viewpoint: on an altar the offering, the immolation and the eating of a victim. We must also consider its purpose. In the *memento* of the living, the Roman Canon describes the Mass as 'a sacrifice of praise'. This description is not intended to be exclusive: it is not saying that the Mass is purely a spiritual sacrifice, consisting of our sentiments towards God. Nor does this phrase seek to deny that the Mass is a redemptive sacrifice, bringing salvation to man at the same time as signifying obedience and expiation before God. While accepting the reality of this sacrifice and its manifold purpose, the fact remains that it is offered in God's praise. In the sacrificial language of the Old Testament, 'sacrifice of praise' could have two meanings. It could be used to describe a very real type of sacrifice, offered on an altar and with something immolated or consumed;[18] it could also be taken as referring to that religious spirit which must accompany every sacrifice if it is to be pleasing to God.[19] When the prophets appear to say that God rejects sacrifices or even abhors them, they want to point out that God takes no pleasure in immolations or offerings that are not inspired by a truly religious spirit.

We can already acknowledge a certain sacrificial value in the Liturgy of the Hours, deriving from and subordinated to the Mass, in so far as this liturgy is the framework within which the Mass takes place. Celebrating the Hours arouses in us that spirit of praise which must be exercised when offering the sacrifice of the Mass.

The word sacrifice can also be employed in a much wider and almost metaphorical sense. This is what St Paul often seems to do. For him, the apostolate may certainly be described as a sacrifice, as a liturgy.[20] He is able to say the same of the faith engendered by his preaching.[21] The same is true of the charitable offering of the Philippians[22] – a use which we should not reduce to the moralistic and even commercial sense which modern language often gives to the word sacrifice, meaning any kind of loss or deprivation in the material or financial order. Finally, St Paul exhorts the Romans to offer a sacrifice which is pleasing to God, in offering him their bodies, by which he means their whole person, the whole of their daily life.[23]

Properly understood, the Liturgy of the Hours may be called a sacrifice in this wider and metaphorical sense. It is however obvious that this is not all we mean when we describe the Liturgy of the Hours as a sacrifice, since in this sense any

18. Cf. Lv 7:12–15. 19. Cf. Ps 49, above all v. 14 and 23.
20. Rom 1:9; 15:16. 21. Phil 2:17. 22. Phil 4:18.
23. Rom 12:1.

activity of the Christian may be considered as a sacrifice.[24] It is admitted that the total consecration signified by religious vows gives the whole of religious life a sacrificial character: not only the contemplative or apostolic activities, but meals and sleep have this character too.[25] No religious, however, would think that he is doing an equally sacred act when he goes into the dormitory as when he goes into choir to celebrate the divine liturgy.

If we want to give the Liturgy of the Hours its exact sacrificial value – neither exaggerated by making it equal to that of the Mass, nor minimized by reducing it to the same level as any other Christian action – we must ask ourselves what exactly we mean by sacrifice. St Thomas defines it as a physical act, a ritual act (by which he means determined by the law of the Church) in which man signifies visibly a homage which can be rendered to God alone.[26]

This visible significance is best realized in the ritual consisting of a bloody immolation, the destruction of something offered: it appears that nothing better expresses the fact that God is our sovereign Master and that we owe him everything. There is no bloody immolation in the Mass, and St Thomas gives a definition of immolation which is wide enough to include unbloody sacrifice as well. For him, there is an immolation when you do something (*aliquid fit*) which shows sufficiently that the offerer wants to do something more than make an ordinary offering: a true sacrifice, expressing a total gift.[27]

If we consider the terms of the definition that we have given, we can see that it applies to the Liturgy of the Hours. This is in fact a physical and visible reality – we use our voices, we take up certain bodily attitudes. The Liturgy of the Hours has been ritualized by the Church, and it has been so arranged and ordered as to be clearly recognizable as a homage to God alone. Even though the Office is sometimes celebrated in the honour and in memory of a saint – just as the Mass may be offered in memory

24. 'For all their (the laity's) works, prayers, and apostolic endeavours, their ordinary married and family life, their daily labour, their mental and physical relaxation, if carried out in the Spirit and even the hardships of life, if patiently borne – all of these become spiritual sacrifices acceptable to God through Jesus Christ (cf. I Pet 2:5) . . . Thus, as worshippers whose every deed is holy, the laity consecrate the world itself to God' (*Lumen Gentium*, art. 34).

25. This is the common doctrine: by the three vows, the religious makes his or her entire life a sacrifice, *S. Th*, 2a – 2ae qu. 186, a. 7.

26. Cf. *S. Th.* 2a – 2ae, qu. 85.

27. *Ibid.*, a. 3, sol. 3.

of our Lady or St Peter, but not to our Lady nor to St Peter – it is always celebrated for the praise of God.

There are other acts in the Christian life that may be called sacrifices in the wide sense, in that they are accomplished for the glory of God. This is because of an ultimate purpose, or a purpose which has been added on to the purpose already there. 'Whatever you eat, whatever you drink, whatever you do at all, do it for the glory of God' (I Corinthians 10:31). That may well be, but the immediate reason for eating and drinking is personal nourishment, while the celebration of the Office has the glory of God as its *proximate*, *immediate end*. That is why those who celebrate the Hours can give unaware observers, or observers whose faith is weak, the impression that they are doing nothing, that they are wasting their time.

Nevertheless, they are doing something, *they are doing something sacred*, which is a wide, but real, definition of sacrifice.[28] What is the material reality that the celebration of the Hours thus transforms into a sacred reality? It is time. The celebration of the Hours is the *consecration of time*. This confirms yet further the view that it is not merely a dose of prayer to be consumed, no matter how, within twenty-four hours. It is the regular, ordered, and rhythmical consecration 'of the whole course of the day'.[29]

What kind of 'time' are we talking about here? We do not mean an abstract and empty measurement, nor something mathematical and impersonal. Time in this context is something concrete, living and personal. It is historical time, which is above all cosmic time following a rhythm of days, nights and seasons. It is biological time, following a rhythm of organic life with its phrases of activity and rest. In reality, the time that we are consecrating in the Liturgy of the Hours *is ourselves*.

Far from being a gratuitous and superfluous 'pastime' for Christians who are well endowed with a sense of poetry and the aesthetic, the celebration of the Liturgy of the Hours is for Christians an *Office*. This means that it is a duty and function of their condition as earthly creatures, who must recognize the sovereign and absolute dominion of their creator by giving him – it seems a pure loss – what is most personal and precious to them.

28. Ibid. 29. CL 84.

Chapter Two

Liturgy[1]

I. The Various Liturgical Hours

1. Introduction to the Whole Office

This introduction consists of three elements:

The versicle: 'Lord open my lips – and my mouth shall declare your praise', which is said while making the sign of the cross on the lips with the thumb.

An invitatory antiphon: this varies in accordance with different days, seasons and feasts, and characterizes each Office. It may be repeated after each strophe of the invitatory psalm.

The invitatory psalm: traditionally this invitatory psalm is Ps 94. Ps 99 or Ps 66 may also be used.

We have spoken of this introduction to the Office on its own, since it is used either before Lauds or before the Office of Readings, depending on which is used to begin the day.

2. Morning Lauds and Vespers

The full name of Lauds is 'morning Lauds (praises)'. It is a curious quirk of language that we should have continued to call the morning Office Lauds, while we used Matins for the night Office, which should really have been called 'nocturns' or 'vigil'. In the present reform Matins has become 'the Office of Readings' (see below n. 3).

The office of morning praise and that of Vespers (from the word which means evening) constitute the two hinges of the Office. According to tradition they are the most important parts of the Office, since they envelop the whole day. These are the two that should be celebrated more solemnly, and if possible they should be sung. If it is not possible to say all the Hours, these are the two that should be given preference.

1. This whole chapter is basically a presentation of the General Instruction on the Liturgy of the Hours from No. 34 onwards; it will be sufficient to make this one reference without referring to that document every time it comes up. We shall however be referring to the *Constitution on the Liturgy* (CL), which the General Instruction puts into effect.

It is to these Hours that the faithful should be more especially invited. Care has been taken to make them as popular as possible by trying to avoid difficult psalms, and by including in them the 'Prayers' and the common recitation of the Our Father.[2]

In celebrating Morning Lauds and Vespers, the Church is not merely celebrating the rising and setting of the sun. Dawn symbolizes the resurrection of Christ who is, as the canticle of Lauds (*Benedictus*) puts it, 'the rising sun'. The Hour of Lauds is therefore a triumphant hour, which looks to the future, not only of our day, but of the life of the world. It often has missionary overtones: we find this once again in the *Benedictus*, which announces the mission of John the Baptist.

The setting of the sun, corresponding to the Hour of Vespers, symbolizes the will and testament of Christ by the institution of the Eucharist at the evening meal, and his death on the cross at 'the hour' of the enemies of Jesus and of 'the powers of darkness' (Luke 22:53), while the sun was hidden (Luke 23:44).

It is then the hour of 'the evening sacrifice' (Ps 140:2) and of the Eucharist – not giving this word its strictly sacramental meaning, but its meaning of thanksgiving for all the gifts received during the day.

Although they have a different character, these two Hours have a similar structure. Like all the Hours, they begin with a hymn. This should be a popular hymn, more easily understood than the psalms. We speak in the conditional here because the work of composing a repertoire of vernacular hymns which are of good literary value, genuinely religious, and popular, will not be achieved in a day!

The arrangement of Psalms in Lauds and Vespers, as in all the other Hours (with the exception of Compline), is such that they fall into three units. In each of them there are only two psalms properly so called. A 'canticle' is added: this is the term used to designate genuine psalms, or hymns of praise, which are found in biblical books other than the Psalter. At Lauds the canticles are from the Old Testament. At Vespers, they are from the New Testament. This explains why they are placed after the psalms at Vespers, but between the psalms at Lauds, so that the order of the two Testaments may be preserved.

The psalms of Lauds were chosen in accordance with a principle long sanctioned by tradition: the first is a morning

2. Cf. CL 89a and 100.

psalm; the last is a psalm of praise, many of them chosen from the psalms at the end of the Psalter which begin with 'praise the Lord' (from Ps 148 and even Ps 145–150). These were always used to end Lauds and were perhaps responsible for the name given to this Hour.

The psalms at Vespers are relatively easy and popular psalms of thanksgiving. When I say relatively, I am thinking of Ps 109, which is very often used at Vespers on Sundays and feast days. This psalm is very rich in content and very concise: not everyone would consider it an easy psalm.

After the psalmody there comes a 'short reading' of the word of God (see below no. 14), which may also be illustrated and given practical applications in a homily.

It is not sufficient to listen to the word of God: we must understand it and assimilate it. A period of silence will therefore be welcome. There follows a short response. Structured as an echo, this facilitates participation even without a book, and offers another way of absorbing the word of God.

The short response is followed by the traditional canticle: at Lauds it is the *Benedictus* (or canticle of Zacharia), and at Vespers it is the *Magnificat* (or canticle of our Lady). As with the Gospel at Mass, one stands for this and crosses oneself. The place of these canticles at Lauds and Vespers reflects their respective characters. They are very similar in so far as they are both songs of thanksgiving containing innumerable references to the Old Testament. They differ in that the *Benedictus* is more orientated towards the future, to the dawn of salvation. The *Magnificat* is also prophetic, but it is a little less missionary in spirit; thanksgiving for the divine promises already brought about is the dominant theme.

At the beginning and end of the canticle there is a variable antiphon which, especially on feast days, gives a new colour or brings out a particular characteristic of the canticle itself.

The Lord's Prayer, solemnly sung by all present, is a particular characteristic of these morning and evening prayers and is their climax. Since it also is found in the Mass, we are thus maintaining the usage already testified by Tertullian in the third century, of saying the Lord's Prayer three times a day.

The Concluding Prayer is then said. It is found in the Psalter for ordinary days and in the Proper for other days. As regards this Proper Prayer, we should remember that when Mass follows Lauds, this prayer is again used as the collect at Mass and one would thus be saying it twice in a very short space of time.

Lauds and Vespers conclude differently, depending on whether or not a priest or deacon presides. If one of these ministers does preside, then he gives the greeting, blessing and dismissal, as at the end of Mass. Otherwise, the person who is presiding concludes each of these Hours with a formula which does not imply authority, but expresses a wish for all present: 'May the Lord bless you . . . Let us bless the Lord. . . .'

3. The Office of Readings

This Hour is the only one which has not retained its former name in the renewal of the Liturgy of the Hours.[3] It corresponds to the ancient 'Matins', which was theoretically a night office, but which, in fact, was generally anticipated in the afternoon or the day before, or even recited whenever one could! This Hour is no longer strictly an 'Hour': it may be recited at any time of the day. It is characterized not by the time at which it is said, but by its content: in this Office, reading takes pride of place.

This does not mean that it should be considered as a sort of didactic interlude in the office of praise. The reading of the word of God, of the Fathers of the Church, or of readings concerning the saints, certainly aim to instruct us, but with a view to prayer. This purpose of the readings is indicated by the responses which follow them.

There are now two readings in this Office: firstly, a biblical reading, and then a patristic or hagiographical reading. These two readings will certainly not be longer than the total of the six readings which were formerly found in Matins. The introduction of 'breviaries', books which could easily be carried around, had led to the chopping and abbreviating of readings in so material a fashion that they had lost a great deal of their interest. Even as far as the scriptures were concerned, the way the readings had been cut or linked together did not help to hold the reader's attention (on the meaning and choice of readings, see below n. 12).

If the Offices of Readings contained nothing else, it would hardly find a place in the liturgy of praise. In point of fact, the

3. The term Middle Hour (cf. no. 5) is also new. It does not replace the names of Terce, Sext and None; rather it embraces them all.

readings are preceded by the invitatory psalm (if you are beginning the Office), the hymn and three psalms, or three sections of a longer psalm. The so-called 'historical' psalms (77, 104, 105), which consist in a religious interpretation of the history of God's people – a meditation on sacred history, have been carefully reserved to the 'principal seasons' of the Church's year (Advent – Christmas – Epiphany and Lent – Eastertide).

The transition from the psalms to the readings is achieved by a versicle that it would be wrong to ignore: its function is to show the link between the prayer of praise and listening to the word.

The Office of Readings concludes – before the prayer proper to the day – with the hymn *Te Deum*. Formerly used almost daily, it is now reserved in exactly the same way as the *Gloria* at Mass to Sundays outside Lent, to Solemnities and Feasts. By restricting its use, its festive character is set in clearer relief. This is further safeguarded by the fact that its final verses, from *Salvum fac populum tuum*, have become optional. These last verses in fact had been added on to the *Te Deum*, and their suppliant and penitential tone was not in harmony with the lyrical enthusiasm of the hymn's opening lines.

4. Vigils

A liturgical reform must remain in the realm of the possible and adapt itself to the realities of modern life: one cannot expect the majority of priests, never mind the laity, to pray regularly during the night. If we want signs, words and times to recover their true significance, we cannot ask those who recite 'Matins' at three o'clock in the afternoon to read:

Nocte surgentes,
vigilemus omnes . . .

So it was wise not to assign the Office of Readings to any particular time of the day. Each person can choose that moment in his day which is best suited for carrying it out calmly. A person will need to have the different lectionaries at hand, and this Office will perhaps demand a little more calm and quiet than the others.

This adaptation to the realities of our situation should not entail the complete suppression of customs which have been so dear to many of the saints, nor should it oblige everyone to accept the lowest common denominator. Prayer during the night has received high recommendation in the literature of the past, and even in the psalms.[4] It has a spiritual significance and a psychological value which are easily recognizable. There is nothing to prevent those who wish to do so giving a nocturnal quality to the Office of Readings. It will therefore have two series of hymns: one will have no reference to the time at which it is being said, while the other will be suited to recitation in the night.

This Office is relatively short. It would be an exaggeration to call it a 'vigil'. It is intended that certain religious, and even all Christians on certain days, should be able to prolong this night prayer in imitation of the Paschal Vigil, 'mother of all vigils'. This optional amplification of the Office of Readings will consist in lengthening certain parts of it. After the normal psalmody and readings, the theme of praise is taken up again by using biblical canticles indicated in the Appendix of the Liturgy of the Hours. On solemnities and feasts, the Gospel of the Mass of the vigil is read or, failing that, the Gospel of the Mass of the day; on Sundays, a paschal Gospel is read as indicated in the Appendix. This last reading may be illustrated and developed in a homily (and with silence). The Office closes with the *Te Deum* and the prayer of the day.

5. The Middle Hour, Terce, Sext and None

From very early times the Christian day has been sanctified by prayers which marked the various stages of this day itself, and not only its beginning and end. In codifying them, undoubtedly under monastic influence, they were designated as Terce, Sext and None, that is to say – in accordance with the ancient compilation which established the 'first hour' at six o'clock in the morning – at nine o'clock, midday and three o'clock in the afternoon. Some of these Hours were certainly Hours of prayer at the temple in Jerusalem. Peter and John healed the cripple at the Beautiful Gate as they went up to the Temple for prayers at the ninth Hour (Acts 3:1).

The Gospels and the Acts of the Apostles have recorded, at each of these three Hours, various events dear to Christian piety. Mark tells us that the crucifixion was at the third hour (Mark 15:25), while John gives the appearance before Pilate as having taken place 'at about the sixth hour' (John 19:14). The three Synoptics say that 'darkness covered the earth from the

4. For example: 1: 2; 15:7; 42:4.9; 118:55; 133:2; 138:12.

sixth to the ninth hour' (Matthew 27:45 and parallels). Matthew and Mark place the death of Our Lord as happening 'at about the ninth hour' (Matthew), and 'at the ninth hour' (Mark).

On the other hand, it is thought that the coming of the Holy Spirit on the day of Pentecost took place at the third hour, because of Peter's words: 'These men are not drunk, as you imagine; why, it is only the third hour of the day' (Acts 2:15). The ascension has been localized at the sixth hour because the ending in Mark (Mark 16:14) attaches it, rather loosely it is true, to a meal of the apostles. In the same way the opening of Acts (Acts 1:4) places the promise of the Spirit, which will soon be followed by the ascension, in the course of a meal shared by Jesus with his apostles.

It is also at the sixth hour that Peter, who was praying and was hungry . . . (Acts 10:9–10) . . . had that vision of a sheet filled with clean and unclean foods which symbolized the entry of the pagans into the Church, in the person of the centurion Cornelius, to whom an angel had appeared on the day before at about the ninth hour (Acts 10:3).

These three Hours are maintained. But for the majority of clergy and faithful, they are replaced by the 'Middle' Hour – so called because it is placed between Morning Lauds and Vespers. Depending on the possibilities of communities or individuals, it may be celebrated at any time in the course of the day.

It includes a hymn, which varies in accordance with the actual time of celebration; three psalms or sections of psalms; a short reading followed by a versicle, and a Concluding Prayer.

Communities or individuals who desire and are able (habitually or occasionally) to say the three Hours of Terce, Sext and None, may do so. They will obviously say them at the corresponding Hour. It would be absurd to return to the practice, which was normal when the three Hours were obligatory for everybody, of lumping them all together into one. It is precisely in order to avoid this that the idea of a Middle Hour was introduced.

If all three Hours are said, then for one of them the psalmody given for the Middle Hour is used. For the other two, the psalmody from the 'gradual psalms' is used.[5] This represents a return to the monastic custom of using these psalms almost every day. Their brevity and their daily repetition allow them to be

5. The psalms 119 to 133.

said at the place of work and from memory, without having to have a book.

The purpose of the Middle Hour – and still more that of Terce, Sext and None – is easy to see. It affords the opportunity of a breathing space in God's presence while we are in the midst of our work, and helps us to sanctify this work without interrupting it too much.

6. Compline

The Latin word *completorium*, which does not seem to have been used before the rule of St Benedict, means: (the Office) which completes, which concludes the Liturgy of the Hours and signals the end of the day. It is not therefore an evening prayer like Vespers, although a number of parishes and communities have substituted Compline for Vespers as if one were equivalent to the other. More precisely, Compline is a prayer to be said before going to bed. It should be the last act of the day, and considering our present habits, can even be said after midnight: it still forms a part of the Office of the day which is about to end.

It is encouraged that the Hour should begin with an examination of conscience. When celebrating Compline in common, this may be done in silence or even by using the formulas given in the Missal for the penitential act.

It begins with the same verse as all the other Hours of the Office (with the exception of the first Hour), and with its own hymn.

Its psalmody is considerably reduced, as well suits people who are tired at the end of the day: there is a single psalm, or two if they are very short.

The psalms given for Sunday Compline may be used on any day of the week. This allows a person to recite Compline from memory, when he comes home late at night for example. To avoid depriving those who use this facility of the psalms given for Compline on the days during the week, these psalms also occur elsewhere in the cycle of the psalter.

The psalms are followed by a short reading, which varies according to the particular day; the response *In manus tuas* follows and then comes the canticle of Simeon, the *Nunc dimittis*, neither of which ever change; a Concluding Prayer is given in the Psalter for Compline of every day of the week.

The Hour comes to a close with the blessing *Noctem quietam*, and an antiphon to the Blessed Virgin Mary.

7. The Link between the Various Hours and the Mass

It often happens when celebrating the Office in common that one of the Hours comes immediately before or after the Mass. Rules are given for the organic union of these two celebrations. This union of the two however, will only be made if there are no pastoral reasons against it. When the faithful, who may be unfamiliar with the Office of Lauds, come to Mass they could be upset for example, by not knowing where Lauds finishes and Mass begins.

To put it briefly, we can say that on ordinary days it is the Hour which has precedence over the beginning or end of the Mass which it precedes or follows; on Sundays and feastdays, it is the Mass with its entrance hymn that has precedence. The Hour, however, always retains its psalmody and the canticle – whether it be the *Benedictus* or *Magnificat*.

Normally – with the exception of Christmas in fact – the Office of Readings and the Mass should remain independent of one another. Each has its own cycle of readings which should retain its particular character.

The *General Instruction*, in which this observation is found, does not mention a link between Mass and Compline. This is undoubtedly because of the informal and almost private character of this Hour.

8. A Panorama of the Reform of the Hours

From what has been said we can see that the general arrangement of the Office has changed little. In order to meet the needs of contemporary life and to ensure a genuine relationship of the Hours to the time of day, the Office of Readings no longer has the character of a night Office. Terce, Sext and None may be replaced by a single Hour: the Middle Hour, which is more easily adapted to different ways of life.

Yet those who wish to maintain the nocturnal character of the Office of Readings – and so make it a genuine vigil – and those who wish to keep Terce, Sext and None, are enabled to do so.

Only one Hour from the former Office has been completely supressed: namely, Prime. Historically this was the latest arrival in the general sequence of Hours. It related to Lauds, much in the same way as Compline related to Vespers. But while the emphasis of modern life on evening and night time made it possible to allow for a reasonable distance between Vespers and Compline, the same phenomenon made Prime a burden. Its suppression had already been decided well before the present reform.[6] The most characteristic aspect of this Hour, namely the consecration to God of the day and of its work, has not only been safeguarded but highlighted by the new Prayers.

Finally, it should be observed that the whole of the reform of which we are speaking concerns those who used the Roman Office: the monastic Office is the object of a separate reform.

II. The Various Parts of the Liturgy of the Hours

9. The Psalms

The entire liturgy is, if not incomprehensible, then at least alien and dull if there is not a minimum of biblical knowledge and taste for the Bible.[7] A particularly striking application of this fundamental law is found in the Liturgy of the Hours, of which the psalms are the backbone. Even the best reform, one well adapted to the rhythm and spirit of modern life, could never dispense with the need to know and relish the psalms if the celebration of this liturgy of praise is to be attractive and fruitful.[8]

Breviaries prior to the present reform seemed designed to discourage attention to the psalms. With the exception of a few more recent editions, they were printed without any title other than their number. Chopped into uniform verses and half-verses, their structure – which would have given an indication to their literary genre – was largely hidden. Above all, the sheer number of psalms to be recited one after another (normally fourteen when Matins and Lauds were said together, not counting the invitatory psalm, the *Te Deum* and the *Benedictus*) fostered rapid recitation and hindered a consideration of each psalm in itself.

6. This was already decided in CL 89d. In fact, Pope Paul VI in his Motu proprio *Sacram liturgiam* of 25 January 1964, No. 7, gave 'to those who are not bound to choir, the possibility of omitting Prime and of choosing from among the other little Hours that which was best suited to the time of the day'.

7. CL 24. 8. CL 90.

A more contemporary and varied typographical lay-out, the emphasis on each psalm by the means that we shall indicate in the following paragraph, the use of the vernacular, and especially the reduction of the number to be said each day and at each Hour: all these things help maintain one's concentration. It will however, not be long before we fall back into routine if we do not make a personal effort to prepare ourselves, to understand and to concentrate on the psalms.

It is impossible to offer a full exposition of the psalms within the limits of this book. It will be well to look for that elsewhere.[9] We limit ourselves to a few rapid reflections.

The understanding of the psalms has its basis in faith. We must first of all believe that the psalms are inspired, that they are the word of God, and, like the rest of the Bible – but in different degrees – a word which calls me, which is addressed *to me today*. The psalms are a special case: it is a word of God which is not spoken to me merely so that I can hear it, but in order that I should say it to him and that I should pray using his own word. Confronted with this wonderful mystery, why should we be worried by the difficulties of detail which we meet in the psalms?

The psalms belong to the Old Testament. Before looking for their spiritual or full sense, we should take their literal sense seriously: what could give us a deeper respect, a greater confidence, or a greater love for God? We can apply to the psalms what the dogmatic *Constitution on Revelation* says of the Old Testament books in general: 'These same books then, give expression to a lively sense of God, contain a store of sublime teachings about God, sound wisdom about human life, and a wonderful treasury of prayers; in them the mystery of our salvation is present in a hidden way. Christians should receive them with reverence.'[10]

As regards this literal sense, we must learn to distinguish the *different literary genres of the psalms*: messianic psalms, historical psalms, sapiential psalms which are alphabetical in structure, royal psalms, hymns of praise, songs of thanksgiving,

9. There is a good exposition in the General Instruction on the Liturgy of the Hours (nn. 100–109). Read also P. Salmon, *L'Office divin*, ch. III: 'De l'interprétation des psaumes dans la liturgie aux origines de l'office'. Cf. also A.-M. Roguet, *Le miel du rocher ou la douceur des Psaumes* (*L'Esprit Liturgique*, 27) Paris, 1967.

10. *Dei Verbum*, 15.

individual or national lamantations. . . . A similarity of vocabulary, and above all routine, tend to hide this variety from us: to know how to recognize it is, however, the first condition for an interesting and wholesome recitation.[11]

The Psalter is not a haphazard collection, nor is it a little island in the ocean of the Bible. It could be called a point of synthesis where all the themes and ideas of the Bible come together and are expressed in poetical form, with love and thanksgiving as the *leitmotif.* There is no book in the Bible – historical, legislative, prophetic, sapiential, evangelical, apocalyptic – which does not find an echo in the Psalter. The more one comes to know and to appreciate the Bible in its unity and in its diversity, the more one will know and savour the psalms – and vice-versa.

The two Testaments form one revelation, unified in the mystery of Christ gradually unfolding in the course of history. That is why even if the psalms are not Christian, and it is pointless to try and Christianize them artificially, they are nevertheless *christological.* This means that they speak of Christ. They announce the Messiah, they are orientated towards him, prophesy his coming and find in him alone their fulfilment. That is why Jesus himself said: 'Everything written about me in the Law of Moses, in the prophets and in the *psalms,* has to be fulfilled' (Luke 24:44).

Not only do the psalms speak of Christ, but Christ himself speaks in the psalms. Not only do the Evangelists apply them to him,[12] but he himself often quotes them applying them to himself, not only in the course of his life,[13] but even at his supreme Hour, that of the Passion.[14] To this historical fact we must add this principle of liturgical theology: 'He is present when the Church prays and sings the psalms.'[15] 'Christ Jesus, high priest of the new and eternal covenant, taking human nature, introduced into this earthly exile that hymn which is sung throughout all ages in the halls of heaven. He joins the entire community of mankind to himself, associating it with his own singing of this canticle of divine praise.'[16] When the Church sings the Hours,

11. Cf. P. Drijvers, *The Psalms,* New York, 1965.
12. Mt 13:34; Jn 2:17; 19:24.
13. Mt 7:23 and parallels; 21:16 and parallels; 21:42 and parallels; 22:44 and parallels; 23:39 and parallels; Jn 10:34.
14. Mt 27:45 and parallels; Lk 22:69; 23:46; Jn 13:18; 19:28.
15. CL 7. 16. CL 83.

'it is the very prayer which Christ himself, together with his body, addressed to the Father'.[17]

'With his body . . .'. *Christ and the Church are one* . . . When we sing the psalms, we are identifying ourselves not only with the personal Christ, but with the whole Christ: this great principle for the interpretation of the psalms was brilliantly illustrated by St Augustine: 'It is truly the voice of the bride addressing her bridegroom. . . . All who perform this service are not only fulfilling a duty of the Church, they are sharing in the greatest honour accorded to Christ's spouse, for by offering these praises to God they are standing before God's throne in the name of the Church their Mother.'[18]

In singing the psalms, *we can identify ourselves with the Church*, the body of Christ, and also with 'the whole community of mankind': not only with the saints, but with sinners, with unbelievers, with all those who struggle and suffer, especially when we pray the psalms which speak of the poor, the persecuted, the wretched. . . .

When we say the psalms in our celebration of the Liturgy of the Hours, *we are in communion with the whole people of God*, and also with the whole of their life, with the whole history of salvation. That helps us to understand how the psalms, embracing as they do that Paschal mystery which throws its light on all aspects of the history of salvation, can, while remaining songs of the Old Testament, allow us to sing of Christian realities such as Baptism, the Eucharist, and the Virgin Mary.[19]

10. Appreciating the Psalms

The faithful are helped to appreciate the psalms by three features in the Liturgy of the Hours, the first two of which were completely lacking in our former breviaries.[20]

First of all, the titles. These state the content of the psalms, their literal meaning. A further phrase, taken from the New Testament or from the writings of the Fathers, is also provided as an indication of the psalms' christological aspect. Although these two indications do not have official value, it is however

17. CL 84. 18. *Ibid.*

19. An official sub-title of the Dogmatic Constitution *Lumen Gentium*, VIII, 2, has the words: 'The Role of the Blessed Virgin in the Economy of Salvation'.

20. At least in the official books of the Roman liturgy. The psalms had titles in the Cistercian breviary, and also in the more recent vernacular breviaries.

permitted in private recitation to substitute the second of these for the liturgical antiphon.

Some *Psalm-collects* are given for each psalm in the Appendix of the Liturgy of the Hours. It represents a return to a very ancient custom.[21] After singing the psalms the monks in ancient times used to prostrate themselves for a period of silent prayer. The president of the assembly concluded this silent prayer with a collect which was intended as a concise summary of the principle themes of the psalms. Some examples of this usage still exist, and are well known by liturgists. Sometimes they are deceptive, since they are a play on the Latin words rather than the deeper themes. Some recent attempts have shown that this method can be very useful in our prayer today.[22]

Finally, in liturgical celebrations each psalm has always been accompanied by an antiphon which precedes it – since, musically, it gives it its tone – and which follows it. It can even be repeated after each strophe of the psalm. Some antiphons, above all those at the *Benedictus* and at the *Magnificat*, are valuable literary compositions although often without any close link with the psalms.[23] The majority of antiphons are however taken from the psalm itself. They are valuable in that they help to indicate the literary genre or to emphasize a thought of particular importance. Moreover, they throw light on the psalm without imposing on it an artificial and extraneous interpretation.

11. The Arrangement of the Psalms

The Hour of Prime has been suppressed; the Office of Readings has only three psalms instead of nine; Lauds has two psalms instead of four; Vespers has two psalms instead of five; the Middle Hour has three, but may replace the three little Hours which had nine psalms altogether; Compline no longer has three, but only one or two. It has been necessary to discard the aim of St Pius X's reform that the entire Psalter should be recited within one week. St Benedict had applied this principle although in a slightly different way, and the monks remained faithful to this. In his Rule their Patriarch had declared (ch.

21. Cf. P. Verbraken, *Oraisons sur les 150 psaumes* (*Lex Orandi* 42), Paris, 1967.

22. We are thinking of the concluding prayers to each psalm, given by J. Gelineau and D. Rimaud in *Le Psautier de la Bible de Jérusalem*, Paris, 1961.

23. It is in this general sense that one speaks, for example, of the 'Marian antiphons', which are independent songs.

18): 'If someone does not find this arrangement of the Psalter to his liking, he may change it – if he finds a better one', but he added: 'Provided that in all events the entire Psalter is recited in the course of a week. . . .'

The Constitution on the Liturgy decided to distribute the one hundred and fifty psalms over a period of time longer than a single week. After studying the question, it was decided to adopt a period of four weeks. We should not conclude from this that from now on we shall be saying four times less psalms! In fact, there have been added to the one hundred and fifty psalms four series of Old Testament canticles at Lauds, which is twice as many as in the former Roman Breviary. At Vespers, a whole new series of New Testament canticles has been introduced.

Besides, we have already observed that the psalms which may be said at the little Hours outside the Middle Hour, and those which are normally said at Compline on weekdays, will also be found in the four-weekly cycle of psalms.

The Office of Readings has two cycles of readings on certain days – for major seasons and for ordinary times of the year. Several of the most outstanding psalms recur a number of times in the course of the four weeks.

When the psalms, even if divided into sections, are too long for a single Hour, they are not continued at the following Hour but are taken up again at the same Hour on the following day. This means that communities and individuals who do not recite all the Hours each day are not therefore obliged to recite bits and pieces of psalms.

This liturgical Psalter contains certain omissions in comparison with the complete Psalter of the Bible.[24] Certain verses, because they express violence or because they curse, have been passed over in silence. Three psalms, in which it was judged that violence was the dominant theme, have been entirely eliminated from the four-week cycle. These are psalms 57, 82 and 108.[25]

It must be acknowledged that this last point raised serious problems. There is a liturgical problem, since traditionally the liturgy has faithfully maintained the complete Psalter of the

24. These omissions are indicated either by references, or in the text.

25. It is true that in the psalm 108, verses 6 to 19 form a litany of maledictions. By omitting them however, as has been done elsewhere, verses 1 to 5, and 20 to 31 – which constitute a magnificent psalm of the poor – could have been retained.

Bible. There is a literary problem: these psalms are poems, in which each forms a whole. There is a double problem of biblical theology: in general terms, since the whole of scripture is inspired; on a particular level, since the psalmist did not curse his personal enemies, but the enemies of God – the psalmist is seized by a 'holy anger'. Those responsible for the reform of the Liturgy of the Hours undoubtedly considered these objections.

While the reform wishes to remain in harmony with tradition, it also wants to adapt itself to present day needs. This will allow the faithful to take part fully in the renewed liturgy. Another factor was taken into account – the use of the vernacular. It is obvious that while theoretical justifications may be found for verses or entire psalms of violence, to say these words aloud or to sing them in our own language has practical difficulties. Saying such words or psalms out loud in the church – where we have come to praise God – can be repugnant to many. We would run the risk of turning faithful away from the Liturgy of the Hours.

12. The Biblical Readings and their Responses

Everyone knows the way in which the Second Vatican Council stressed the primary importance of the word of God in revelation, in preaching, in the liturgy, and the spiritual life of priests and faithful.[26]

Quite naturally therefore, the Liturgy of the Hours, as it has always done, gives a special place to the reading of the scriptures. This is the essential characteristic of the Office of Readings. Even if the entire Bible is not read at this Hour, at least its main passages are read in a carefully arranged order, taking into account both the chronological order of the texts, and the traditional affinity of certain books to particular liturgical seasons.

The lectionary for this liturgy is evidently different from that of the Mass. The people working on the two lectionaries have taken pains to avoid having passages coincide at the same time. The lectionary for the Office is twofold: one, on a one-year cycle, is that given in the Liturgy of the Hours. The other is drawn up according to a two-year cycle and therefore offers a richer variety of texts; this second lectionary is found in the Appendix

26. CL 24, 35a; *Dogmatic Constitution on Revelation*, 25; *Decree on the Ministry and Life of Priests*, 4, 18, 19.

of the book of the Hours. There is a further difference between the Mass lectionary and that of the Office which reflects their liturgical usage: the readings at Mass, which are in groups of two or three, are shorter than those of the Office; there is only one biblical reading, and it is of a reasonable length. It is also possible to use more difficult texts in the Office than at Mass; moreover, the biblical readings of the Office of Readings are never drawn from the Gospels.

In order to help the reader or listener to turn his reading into prayer, the biblical passage from the Office is followed by a response. Taken from existing breviaries, or newly composed for the purpose, this response takes a particularly rich and striking phrase which has just been read. It then juxtaposes to this an extract from another biblical book, often from the other Testament, which brings out the implications and nuances of the first text. It is clear that the responses were originally intended to be sung. However, this arrangement is so helpful for prayer that it was decided to retain it even for individual recitation of the Office. Certain repetitions are omitted in individual recitation.

The ecclesiastical reading, coming after the biblical reading, is likewise followed by a response, but a response less tied to the text just read. The short readings at Lauds and Vespers are followed by a short response which, while having the same structure, consists of much shorter phrases. The short responses are thus easier to use with a simple melody.

13. The Ecclesiastical Reading

The second and last reading in the Office of Readings is normally a patristic text. Those preparing this lectionary have drawn on the immense riches in the writings of the Fathers. At the same time care has been taken to select texts which remain of value for people today. Besides the official lectionary of the Roman Church there will be an optional lectionary, which thus increases the area of choice. This will be still further enlarged by the possibility given to episcopal conferences to add to this optional lectionary texts which are better adapted to the mentality and culture of their region.

On the feasts of saints a hagiographical reading will be offered. This will be an extract from the works or authentic words of the saint; or a patristic text which praises him or can well be applied to him; or even a résumé of his life, but in accordance with the demands of historical science and seeking to portray the particular role of this saint in the history of the Church.

Finally, as the people's Missals have done for a long time, the Hours' book will give a brief hagiographical note for the information of the user, but not intended for liturgical recitation.

14. The Short Readings

Generally called the 'capitulum', the former texts for the short readings were very often insignificant either because of their excessive brevity or their too frequent repetition.

The new Liturgy of the Hours offers a large number and a very great variety of short readings, taken from all the biblical books with the exception of the Gospels. There is thus less risk that routine will render them dull and lifeless. The value of these readings is very considerable since their brevity has the advantage of throwing into relief a profound or striking phrase which only too easily passes unnoticed in the course of a longer and more complex reading.

15. The Prayers

This is without doubt the feature which will strike many as an innovation in the new Liturgy of the Hours. The Roman Breviary also had some *preces* of supplication. However, these were hardly more than a fossil. Largely penitential in character and with an unchanging formula, they were only used on particular ferial days at certain times of the year. We have here a profound restoration in the most positive sense of the word,[27] somewhat like that of the bidding prayers in the Roman Mass, which survived in an almost unrecognizable fashion in the form of the *Kyrie* and litanies. This parallel is justified since the General Instruction on the Liturgy of the Hours explains both this renewal and the duty of linking supplication with praise, by

27. It is only fitting to point out the example given on this point by the *Office de Taizé*, on which one can read the presentation by Max Thurian in Cassien-Botte, *La Prière des Heures*, (Semaine Oecuménique de l'Institut Saint-Serge, *Lex Orandi* 35) Paris, 1963.

quoting the text from St Paul (1 Timothy 2:1–4) which the *Constitution on the Liturgy* had also referred to in its decision to restore the bidding prayers at Mass.[28]

On the other hand, there are important differences between the Prayers of the Faithful at Mass, and the *preces* of the Hours. In the first place, the Prayer of the Faithful is a pure prayer of intercession, while the Prayers at Lauds and Vespers, and above all at Lauds, have an important element of 'confession', namely the acknowledgement of the glory of God and the proclamation of our faith, on which we base our hope of being heard. The Prayer of the Faithful at Mass contains intentions addressed to the community, to which the community respond with a simple and uniform invocation. This structure is not applicable to individual recitation. The Prayers at Lauds and Vespers are therefore addressed to God. They can also be divided into two sections, the first being said by the president and the second by the community which has the texts before it. The person saying the Office alone says the whole formula himself. If so desired, the community can leave the entire formula to the president, and limit itself to repeating a simple invocation given at the beginning.

The general framework of these intentions is almost the same at Mass as it is at Lauds and Vespers: the general intentions for the world and the Church, for temporal rulers, for those in need, and for the community.

The Prayers at Lauds have a special object, which they have taken over from the old Hour of Prime: to consecrate to God the day which is about to begin, together with all that it will bring.

The Prayers of Vespers stress thanksgiving. Besides this, they always include an intention for the deceased, replacing the *Fidelium* verse which formerly concluded all the Hours of the Office.[29]

There is a further difference from the Prayer of the Faithful at Mass, in that the Prayers of Lauds and Vespers allow for the insertion of special intentions. The reason for this is easy to understand: the community which celebrates the Office is normally smaller and more homogeneous than that which celebrates Mass.

28. Cf. CL 53.

29. The prayers at Lauds are above all invocations; those of Vespers are above all intercessions. That is why we have preferred not to call them both by the name 'prayers of intercession', but quite simply 'prayers'.

16. Singing[30]

The Liturgy of the Hours is not just a devotional exercise: it is a liturgical celebration. It engages the whole man, with his body, his breath and all his movements. It is in the nature of the liturgy that it should be worship by a community, and this explains the importance attributed to singing: it is not a superfluous trimming but an almost essential need. This is still more true of the Liturgy of the Hours, in which the overriding theme, as we said at the beginning, is praise and thanksgiving. Its most important parts are therefore the psalms, canticles and hymns, namely the emotive and lyrical elements. These find their natural expression in song.

The songs and singing we have in mind are not 'monolithic'. For too long now the attitude on this question, as regards both the Mass and the Office, has been that we should have *all or nothing*. Either everything was sung, which was often difficult and could not be done without a fairly skilled choir – resulting in a tendency for the choir to monopolize the singing and prevent any participation on the part of the faithful – or else, in the absence of a choir, nothing was sung (the 'low Masses'!) and the liturgy was reduced to a joyless recitation – when it was not just a murmur or a hurried mutter.

Different parts of the liturgy need to be sung in a different way. The singing of the psalms for example, should be based on their verse structure. What is more, it is not necessary to sing everything. Certain psalms, for instance those which are meditative and sapiential rather than lyrical, may simply be read by one person alone, as with any biblical passage. The readings, which aim to instruct, gain nothing from being sung. We can also say this for the intentions of the Prayers, and of the Collects. The first requirement of the Prayers is that they should be understood, while the well-known acclamations of response almost cry out to be sung.

There are not only objective reasons for rejecting the theory of all or nothing. There are also good reasons of liturgical pedagogy. When encouraging the people to sing, we should not expect them to be capable of singing everything: to start with, they should sing what they can. Then too, the principle of

30. The whole of this paragraph presents nn. 267 to 284 of the General Instruction on the Liturgy of the Hours. They themselves are an application of the rules given in the Instruction *Musicam sacram* on music in the liturgy, issued by the S. Congregation of Rites, 5 March 1967.

'progressive solemnization' requires a gradation between various celebrations: it is normal to sing more at a major Hour and on a solemnity, than at the Middle Hour and on an ordinary day of the week.

17. Attitudes and Gestures

It is fitting to speak of these as elements in the Liturgy of the Hours, since, as we said with regard to singing, the liturgy should engage the activity of the whole man in the community celebration. The rules given on this point are sober: there is a sign of the cross at the beginning of the Hours and for the *Benedictus* and *Magnificat*; everyone stands for the two canticles just mentioned, for the hymn and for the short responses; sitting is the normal posture for listening to the readings. The rest is a question of local custom. Even what might seem self-evident to us is not always acceptable in other parts of the world. In the Far East for example, sitting can be considered more dignified than standing.

18. Freedom of Choice

In what we have already said, you will have noticed the considerable degree of freedom given in arranging the Liturgy of the Hours: the choice of time for saying the Office of Readings and the Middle Hour, the use of the various optional lectionaries, the intermittent use of singing, etc. The General Instruction on the Liturgy of the Hours devotes an entire paragraph to enumerating other possibilities for ample and abundant choice.[31] On reading it you might ask whether any of the regulations expounded above still remain binding and whether such a fluid liturgy, with so many *ad libitum* choices, still merits the name of liturgy?

We must first of all remember that there are limits to this freedom of choice. There is a great degree of liberty on weekdays during the year. The choice is more limited however on Sundays and solemnities, as well as during major seasons of the Church's year which, because of their particular characteristics, have their own special arrangement. Moreover, the freedom of choice

31. Nn. 245–253. The General Instruction on the Roman Missal had already had an entire chapter entitled: 'On choosing the Mass and its various parts' (Ch. VII, nn. 313–325).

is given within a stable framework: the content of the liturgical books, the structure of the Hours, etc.

Many still feel that all liturgy should be strictly predetermined. They consider that what is not formally prescribed is therefore strictly forbidden, and that all communities and congregations in the universal Church should make the same gestures and say the same words in the same language. We must understand that this authoritarian conception of the liturgy, a liturgy where all is uniform, has been formally rejected by the Second Vatican Council.

The Council's reform has sought to be pastoral and pedagogical. It has sought to make the liturgy supple, so that it should once again become and remain a living reality. It was the Council's intention that there should be a certain plurality in the liturgy so as to permit all peoples of the earth to take part in it in accordance with their culture, their traditions and their sensibilities. That is why the Council has taken the revolutionary decision to give a real authority in liturgy to national and regional Conferences of bishops, and even, to a lesser degree, to each bishop in his diocese – where he is the principal celebrant. While not creating his own liturgy, every celebrant enjoys a considerable liberty in choosing its various elements.

Can it be said that with such elasticity, the liturgy retains its unity? That it remains the worship of the universal Church, in which Christ himself is present? Certainly it does, as long as we do not confuse unity with uniformity. Those who celebrate the liturgy in this diversity act liturgically: first of all because they have the intention to do so, and then too because they avail themselves of this liberty within the structures and laws established by the Church herself. Moreover, these faculties are given them by liturgical law itself: these are not irregularities, exceptions, nor just the utilization of indults or dispensations – it is the observation of the law itself, which is certainly a law, but a law of liberty.

In the past, it was a little consolation when a liturgy did not seem adapted to local needs, to say that it was celebrated in exactly the same way in Rome, in Spain, in Africa and in Oceania. It is certainly preferable to use the facilities for adaptation which we now have, not for the pleasure of 'not doing like everyone else', or merely to satisfy personal tastes and whims, but in order to ensure for the assembled congregation, if we are responsible for it, the possibility of a relatively easy participation, so that it feels at ease in the community celebration.

19. Silence

The Constitution on the Liturgy recommended that 'at the proper time all should observe a reverent silence',[32] in order to promote not only an active but also a profound participation by the faithful in the liturgy. This recommendation is now more clearly determined in the rubrics of the Roman Missal.[33] The Liturgy of the Hours, precisely because it consists of words and songs, also has this need for silence. This is another example of the liberty of which we have just spoken – the more so since no moments of silence are laid down in the Liturgy of the Hours. At the end of each psalm, for example, one could have a period of recollection, and likewise at the end of the different readings, whether they are long or short. Only too often, masters of ceremonies and leaders of song seemed to have looked on the liturgy as a sort of implacable machine: once set in motion it no longer has any right to stop. Silence in a liturgical gathering seemed as alarming as a breakdown on a car racing circuit.

We must avoid falling into the opposite excess. An indiscriminate multiplication or prolongation of silences, either during the Mass or during the Hours, runs the risk of boring those taking part. The celebration would cease to be something popular and alive. You would not know whether it was a liturgical celebration or a meditation broken up with song. Nevertheless, a measured degree of silence in the Liturgy of the Hours allows each person to make his or her own what has been heard and sung. It enables interior liberty to coexist with the active participation of a community; it allows external praise to be deepened in adoration. In short, that unity between the liturgical life and contemplation which people often find difficult, will be fostered by the liturgical celebration itself.

If silence is recommended in community celebrations, the same is true in personal recitation, where in fact it is more easily achieved. Certainly, we should not confuse private prayer and the Office. A calm and unhurried celebration of the Office

32. CL 30.

33. General Instruction on the Roman Missal: 23, 32, 88, 121. *The Order of Mass with the People*, 3, 6, 140.

however, with pauses to savour the verse of a psalm or a nourishing thought found in one of the readings, prepares and leads us to personal prayer. In their Rule, the monks in former days did not have 'times for prayer' but they loved to round out the celebration of the Office with silent prayer.

Chapter Three

Spirituality

'Spirituality' is a useful word, but a vague one. It does not describe a particular discipline or doctrine, but a way of looking on divine, sacramental, and ecclesial realities. There has already been a certain 'spirituality' in the preceding pages. The outline we have given of the nature of praise, and of the presence of Christ in the praying community; our brief glance at the psalms and our reflections on the value of singing and silence; all these things touch closely on the ways to Christian perfection. When we read the whole of the General Instruction on the Liturgy of the Hours, we glean many more suggestions for the spiritual and apostolic life. This is one of the characteristics of the present liturgical renewal: it is no longer codified in dry lists of rubrical do's and don'ts. It gives rules and norms which are explained in proportion to their meaning and value on the pastoral and on the spiritual level.

Although this entire Commentary seeks to illustrate the 'spirituality' of the Liturgy of the Hours, it would be useful to offer further spiritual reflections on the Hours taken as a whole.

1. Fruitful Participation

'Participation' is the key-word in the whole of the liturgical renewal. The fundamental idea which it denotes is intimately linked with the ecclesiology of the Council. The Church is not in the first instance a hierarchy, any more than the liturgy is first and foremost the action of the hierarchy: it is the action of the whole of the Church, of the whole body of Christ. The active subject of the liturgy is the holy people of the baptized, and not just the clergy, although these have an important role to play by service and by presiding (at the same time, to preside is in itself a service). No one should be a spectator, all should offer their active participation.

1. The Qualities of Active Participation

The expression dates from St Pius X.[1] It was taken up again by Pius XI[2] and Pius XII broadened and deepened its meaning.[3] This same pope associated with it the idea of *conscious participation*.[4] It is not sufficient to carry out the prescribed rites externally, or in a mechanical way. Their celebration requires a spiritual activity; not passive and resigned as if acquitting oneself of an unpleasant duty, but an activity which is in some way creative. Cassian shows that the monk who is truly familiar with the psalms is not content just to recite them: he has so made them his own that in a way he creates them, he sings them as if they came from himself, as expressing his spirit.[5]

Spiritual does not mean semi-human. Liturgical participation should be *total* participation.[6] We should give ourselves body and soul to the prayer of the Hours, by our words, by our singing and by our physical movements. It is not sufficient to listen, nor to follow with the eyes, nor to say the psalms with one's lips. One can try and correct members of the choir who sing out of tune, but one never has the right to condemn them to silence.

2. Community and Hierarchical Participation

Participation by persons who are not pure spirits but human beings of flesh and blood, should therefore be participation in *community*.[7] This means that we do not participate as individuals who just happen to have come together or are obliged to be together. We celebrate the liturgy as members of an organic community. This implies that we should not think it necessary to do everything ourselves. 'To participate' means that each one should play his or her part. Each person has his or her role in contributing to the harmony of the whole, like different parts

1. The Motu proprio *Tra le sollecitudini* of 22 November 1903. In fact, it concerned the question of the participation of the people in the Offices through Gregorian chant.

2. *Divini cultus* of 20 December 1928, for the 25th anniversary of Pius X's *Motu proprio*.

3. The Encyclical *Mediator Dei* of 20 November 1947. It was from this document that the idea of 'active participation' came to be accepted as a guiding criterion in liturgical renewal.

4. Address to the International Congress for Pastoral Liturgy at Assisi, 22 September 1956.

5. *Conférences* II (*Sources chrétiennes* 54), pp. 92–93.

6. Cf. CL 14, 21, 41.

7. Cf. CL 21, 26, 27.

in one body, like an instrument in a symphony, an actor in a play. We do not participate merely by acting, speaking or singing: we also participate by keeping quiet, by waiting, or by listening when it is the time for someone else to act or to speak.

We have insisted on this point because, for many, the long habit of celebration in private has caused the communal character of the Liturgy of the Hours to disappear from view.[8] Some, in fact, even when they are celebrating in common, continue themselves to say what should be distributed among the various participants.

We have already pointed out earlier[9] that the community celebration of the Office is a good example of true celebration. Eucharistic concelebration is not a bundle of individual celebrations which are private and complete in themselves; it is a single celebration, in which the different concelebrants take part in various and unequal ways. In the same way, in the communal celebration of the Liturgy of the Hours each of the participants should only play his proper role: neither more (for then he would destroy the hierarchical character of the liturgy), nor less (for then he would not be taking part in a sufficiently active way). The priest, religious or lay person who recites the Liturgy of the Hours alone is obliged to say everything, but his solitary celebration is based on celebration in common which is the ideal. In the same way the priest who celebrates Mass alone celebrates in a way which derives from celebration of the Mass with a congregation, rather in the way that one speaks of the 'adaptation' of a symphony for the piano. However, the liturgical rules, in accordance with common sense, authorize the person who celebrates alone – be it Mass or the Liturgy of the Hours – to omit the dialogues, the blessings, and certain other parts (for example the refrains) which are scarcely suited for individual celebration.

This hierarchical aspect of the community celebration with its distribution of roles also follows from a healthy ecclesiology. We are all members of the whole people of God. This community of people is not a shapeless aggregate; it is organized. The work is thus divided, and there is a multiplicity of functions and charisms. This fundamental truth is clearly in evidence in the Office where the various roles are distributed: there are two choirs, a president, cantors, readers, etc.

8. Cf. CL 23. 9. *La Maison-Dieu* 35 (1953), p. 74.

Singing is obviously closely connected with this community aspect of the celebration: it unifies and harmonizes the voices considerably better than does a simple recitation. Where there is that 'progressive solemnization' of which we spoke above, singing has the advantage of bringing out various lights and shades in the celebration, emphasizing the more solemn feasts or the most important parts of the Office. Simple recitation on the other hand, especially in private, tends to produce a dull and uniform celebration, which can only too easily bring boredom, distraction and routine.

3. Easy Participation?

We must try and make participation as easy as possible. In several places *The Constitution on the Liturgy* speaks of *easy* participation.[10] Let us make no mistake: profound participation always demands an effort. But it is still necessary that the complications or obscurities in the liturgy should not aggravate the difficulties unnecessarily. This is the true reason for the simplifications and clarifications brought by the liturgical reform: they are not to be attributed to a lack of fervour or just to empty demagogy. As regards the Liturgy of the Hours, we should be grateful for all those ameliorations which genuinely facilitate participation. The excessive number of Hours often led to their being 'lumped together' by those who had plenty to do. The superabundance of psalms often meant that they were recited too quickly. How could one be attentive, for example, to the various literary genres, when nine psalms were recited at a time (with Matins, or with the three little Hours said altogether)? If the sheer quantity has been reduced this should not be seen either as the effect or the cause of mere slackening, but as demanding better quality, by making this vocal and community prayer lighter and more spacious – giving us room to breathe, we might say. If we make judicious use of silence, our participation in the Liturgy of the Hours should be more pure and more spiritual. It should prepare and facilitiate our prayer, as well as brightening and nourishing it.

4. Fruitful Participation

If our participation has all the qualities of which we have just spoken, then it will be '*fruitful*'. This adjective deserves a

10. Cf. CL 21, 34, 50.

brief comment.[11] Sometimes, pastors have involved the faithful in active participation as if they must do so as their duty, whatever the cost. As far as the Liturgy of the Hours is concerned, as we shall see in a moment, the idea of obligation was so emphasized among clerics that scarcely anything more than an idea of its meritorious value remained. However, the essential value of participation cannot consist in the renunciations and constraints that it imposes upon us, even if these do have a value by reason of the virtues of religion and obedience. The primary purpose of participation in the liturgy is the glory of God. By that very fact, it is profitable to us and to our advantage. It nourishes us with the word and life of God, it unites us to him, it delights us with his love. At the same time, it opens out our hearts to the unlimited dimensions of the heart of Christ and to his intentions for the universal Church and for the whole of mankind. By celebrating the Liturgy of the Hours we undoubtedly carry out our duty, but it is a duty which is our vocation and which, therefore, taken as a whole, should sanctify us and deepen our joy.

5. Obstacles to Participation

This, however, is easier said than done. While participation has become less difficult from the point of view of texts, of rites and of the number and structure of the Hours, it meets a good number of obstacles in us. Routine is always a difficulty we face. If the renewal of the Office, and particularly perhaps the possibility of celebrating it in our mother language, has swept aside routine, this will only last for a time. Once the first impression of novelty has passed away, it will soon return. If we want to avoid routine, we must continually renew our effort to keep our faith, concentration, and recollection alive. This is obvious when you think about it.

We shall dwell for a moment on the theme of recollection. This is often conceived in a manner which, because it is utopian and inhuman, is consequently unattainable. It is sometimes conceived as if it meant emptying our heart and imagination of everything that is foreign to God, in order to concentrate on what is purely sacred. Yet the word 'recollection' brings to mind something entirely different from this empty 'cleansing

11. The adjective itself is only found in CL 11, but the idea is expressed in articles 14, 21, 33, 48, 59, 60, 61, 90, 94, 102, 105. See also LH 14.

process'. It refers to the drawing together of our thoughts, of our desires and of our various affections in order to direct them towards God. When a woman has a child gravely ill, you cannot ask her to forget her concern when she begins to pray. Far from being alien to her prayer, it constitutes its very tissue, its substance. Without it her prayer would be cold and unreal. But her anguish must become prayer through her confidence in God, in faith and hope. Participation in the Liturgy of the Hours in no way obliges us to cast aside our spiritual anguish, the demands of our work, and the preoccupations of our apostolate. It is good that we should take them with us into our liturgical prayer, but in order to put them before God, to unite them to the prayer of Christ and his Church, and to link them with his paschal mystery.

6. Harmony of Mind and Voice?

There is a further difficulty which obstructs a full and fruitful participation. The General Instruction quite rightly quotes the precept of St Benedict: *Mens concordet voci*, Let the Spirit harmonize with the voice, or if you prefer: Let your mind and heart be at one with the words that the liturgy puts in your mouth.[12] Now, we cannot say sincerely, every time the liturgy urges us to do this, that, even in the early morning, we 'cry with joy',[13] or that we are going 'to dance for the Lord',[14] when perhaps we are feeling half asleep and in a thoroughly disagreeable mood! A little later perhaps we find ourselves having to say: 'I am worn out with groaning, every night I drench my pillow and soak my bed with tears; my eye is wasted with grief . . .'[15]

It is impossible to find perfect harmony between spirit and voice with sentiments which are so extreme and which follow one another so rapidly. If we then begin to lose interest in the Office or to consider it as a formality, if we begin to be a mere spectator, what participation will there be?

This is a real difficulty, and we shall only find a solution to it if we deepen our understanding of the mystery of participation. It is in fact a mystery of the ontological and ecclesiological order

12. *Rule*, ch. 19. This adage is quoted, but en passant and without reference, in CL 11 and 90. In LH, the whole of article 19 deals with this point.
13. Ps. 94, with which the entire liturgical day begins.
14. Ps. 34:9. 15. Ps 6:7–8.

and not simply a question of human sentiment and will. Participation is not a sort of picnic, where each person brings along his own provisions. If this were the case, then when I have nothing of particular value to contribute, either because I am not capable of singing, or because at any given moment I cannot associate with a particular flood of sentiments, I would let the celebration develop without me, merely participating with my lips and the occasional ejaculation. I would then be performing an act of devotion. This may be a pious and meritorious action, but it is foreign to the liturgy. The liturgy is not just the sum of individual contributions. It is the act of the people of God as such.

Each person brings what he can, and above all, his attention. It is this that will permit the word of God such as it is, and the Liturgy of the Hours such as the Church has arranged them, to nourish and to form the faithful who participate in it. The Liturgy of the Hours never finds us perfectly ready. It is there to form us little by little: it brings about a continuing education, a constant renewal. Without it we find ourselves in a vicious circle: judging ourselves to be poorly adapted to the liturgy – or feeling that it is not adapted to us, such as we are *hic et nunc* – we do not make it our own, we keep our distance. It becomes impossible for the Office to teach us and to adapt us to itself. Consequently, we shall remain strangers to it. Perhaps because we are bored and convinced that after so long it can bring us nothing, we shall perhaps become more and more alienated from it.

No, we must come to the celebration with a faith which is alive and awake: a general faith with regard the divine mysteries, but also a particular faith in the mystery of the liturgy itself. I myself am this mystery, when I participate in liturgical celebrations, a sacrament of the people of God. This is still more true of the community with whom I celebrate the Hours.

The celebrant of the Liturgy of the Hours, besides myself and my group, is therefore the whole Church. At every moment the universal Church is joyful and radiant, overflowing with praise and thanksgiving, because she is saved and holy. At the same time, this Church, and still more the whole of humanity which she represents, which she attracts, and which she has been sent to save, consists of sinful men. This same Church is therefore suffering and anguished, and all the psalms of lamentation are sung by her without any restriction or dilution.

Furthermore, when the Church is gathered together and sings the psalms, Christ is there with her and sings with her voice. Christ, in his members and in the memorial of his passion is humiliated, anguished, suffering for sinners. At the same time as the Lord, he is living, free, triumphant, glorious, blessing and eternally glorifying the Father.

What is true of celebration in community is also true of individual celebration. Even this is a participation. If the sentiments expressed in the whole Office of praise, but especially in the psalms – be they of lamentation or of rejoicing – are not those of my individual *self*, with my particular personality and changing moods, they are those of my baptismal *self*, as a member of Christ and of the people of God, Temple of the Holy Spirit.

II. Obligation and Freedom

'Talk and behave like people who are going to be judged by the law of freedom' (James 2:12).

To past generations the most marked characteristic of the 'breviary' was that it was obligatory. According to the doctrine commonly held by moralists, for a cleric in major orders the omission of a single 'little Hour' objectively constituted a serious sin. This insistence on obligation should above all have emphasized the importance of the duty of praising God together with the rest of the Church. But in fact this obligation was not considered as the sign or indication of a profound reality. In a way it was sufficient unto itself. The concern of many priests was *to have said* their breviary, a nagging worry which largely destroyed the joy of having it to say at all. Can one freely address oneself to poetry each day under pain of mortal sin? Many would not go to bed at any price without having recited – often one after another and beginning at eleven o'clock at night – all the Hours of the day. This obligation was a daily dose, often swallowed whole and as a homogeneous mass. There was no 'obligation' (apart from the urgings of common sense) to say the Hours at a time at least approximating to the hour at which their name suggested. People felt no scruple in saying them at any old time, in saying words which contradicted the time at which they were being said, and in 'lumping together' so many psalms that it was impossible to say them intelligently and with devotion. The *psallite sapienter*[16] was a beautiful motto, but hardly practised.

It is easy to see the harm that this quantitative and juridical approach can do: it makes the Office a rather unpleasant burden for priests who do not have a very lively appreciation of the liturgy. It could hardly be expected to give them the desire to celebrate the Office calmly and with the desirable intervals. By stressing the importance of the quantity to be said it led to a neglect of the quality of the prayer.

The insistence on this daily obligation for the clergy also had the effect of alienating the laity from the breviary. By saying it they would have adopted a practice which was considered to be reserved to the clerical and monastic caste.

Finally and above all, whatever its psychological effects, one might well ask if legalism of this kind is genuinely Christian, and if it would harmonize with the Pauline doctrine of freedom as found particularly in the letter to the Galatians.

Happily we do not find this 'mentality of slavery' in the new Instruction on the Liturgy of the Hours. Obligation is mentioned, but in a discreet way and as the corollary of a whole doctrine of the prayer of the Church, while the old morals manuals scarcely spoke of the Divine Office except from the angle of obligation and in order to measure its seriousness.

Should we conclude that the celebration of the Liturgy of the Hours has become optional, and that there is now no longer any law on the subject? On this point we must consider what the words law and obligation mean for the Christian.

7. Christian Law

One can obviously consider law as emanating from the will of a superior in order to oblige the subject to obey, without being concerned with the motives or the purpose of the law. This would then be a categorical imperative which did not have to be justified or explained. But this voluntaristic, arbitrary and tyrannical conception of law is not acceptable for the Christian. Even divine law does not constrain us in this way, nor treat us

16. Ps 46:8.

as slaves: it treats us as sons and daughters. The new law is not engraved in stone; it is written in our hearts by the finger of God, by the Holy Spirit.[17] It is a law of love, a law of liberty. This does not prevent it being a law. Christ did not come to abolish the Old Law but to perfect it, which means both to put it in men's hearts and to make it more demanding. While bringing that truth which makes us free it continues to treat us as servants who must obey. If we want to follow it, it even demands of us that we take up our cross each day. The liberty of the Christian must not be used as a cloak and pretext for licence, for disorder or for the view that 'anything goes'.[18]

The law of liberty is therefore far more demanding than a law of constraint, although it is infinitely more bearable. The yoke of Christ does not crush or wound as ordinary yokes do – 'my yoke is easy', but it is nevertheless a yoke. His burden is easy: this is paradoxical for a burden: it is nevertheless a burden.

This is due to the fact that this law is not imposed from outside, it is not a 'categorical imperative'. It comes from within, it is an expression of the nature of things. In this respect the moral 'law', and the supernatural 'law' itself is not without its analogy to physical 'laws'.

The Liturgy of the Hours is regulated by a law of this kind and the General Instruction devotes considerable space to law and obligation understood in this sense.

8. The 'Obligation' of the Liturgy of the Hours

The first lines of the first article state that the 'public and communal prayer of the people of God is rightly considered among the first duties of the Church'. Jesus has commanded us to pray as he did himself, and he has taught us the necessity of prayer (n. 5).

It is man's duty to 'acknowledge and confess the dominion of his creator over him. This is what holy men have done in every age through prayer' and this is through Christ 'the Lord of all men, the one Mediator' (n. 6).

Through baptism we share in the priesthood of Christ so that our new nature as members of Christ unites us with his prayer which 'in the name of and for the salvation of the entire

17. S. Th. 1a–2ae, q. 106, art. 1.
18. Cf. 1 P 2:16; Ga 5:13; Rm 6:15.

human race, he continues to address to his Father in the whole Church and in all her members' (n. 7).

This prayer is inspired and unified by the Holy Spirit, the spirit of Jesus, who is the new law, and who prays in us (n. 8).

Consequently, 'the example and command of the Lord and his apostles to persevere in continuous prayer *are not to be considered a mere legal rule*. Prayer expresses the very essence of the Church as a community' (n. 9).

If this prayer is distributed over certain Hours of the day, it is in order to obey as far as possible the command of Christ to 'pray without ceasing' (nn. 10 and 11).

The Liturgy of the Hours is not a secondary and optional activity of the Church, it is a vital activity. Those who share in her prayer 'make the Lord's people grow by imparting to them a hidden apostolic fruitfulness.' On the other hand 'the readings and the prayers of the Liturgy of the Hours *constitute the source of the Christian life*' (n. 18).

Nevertheless, if the whole of the Church and therefore the whole body of the faithful, has a certain obligation to the Liturgy of the Hours by reason of her nature, it concerns some of her members in a special way.

It regards especially those 'communities . . . obliged by their rule or by their constitution to pray the Liturgy of the Hours.' The profound reason for this is given: those communities 'represent the Church at prayer in a special way . . . they more fully show and fulfil the duty of working, especially by prayer, for "the building up and increasing of the whole mystical Body of Christ" '.

We come finally to the question of individual obligations arising from the particular role of some in the Church, which even as a body is called to the Office of praise: 'The Liturgy of the Hours is entrusted to sacred ministers in a special way so that it is to be recited by each of them – with the necessary adaptations – even when the people are not present. The Church deputes them to the Liturgy of the Hours in order that at least through them the duty of the whole community may be constantly and continuously fulfilled . . .' (n. 28).

This is not an obligation to say an undifferentiated block of Hours. Certainly, they 'will say daily the complete cycle' of the Liturgy of the Hours, but 'observing, as far as possible, the genuine relationship of the Hours to the time of day'.

These various Hours are also enumerated in an order of decreasing importance: firstly, the Hours of Lauds and Vespers, 'which are like the hinges of this liturgy'. These cannot be 'omitted, unless for serious reason'.

The Office of Readings, and its importance is that 'it is above all the liturgical celebration of the word of God', and is therefore particularly important for those who have to hand on that word to others.

Finally, 'they will desire to recite the Middle Hour and Compline, thus commending themselves to God and completing the entire "Opus Dei" before going to bed' (n. 29).

We can see then that the *obligation* of the Liturgy of the Hours is in no sense suppressed. Instead of being presented in terms of compulsion as if it emanated from an arbitrary and overriding law, it is expressed in terms of an essential need. It is in the nature of the Church to celebrate the Liturgy of the Hours. It is something which pertains to the entire Body of Christ, to the whole people of the baptized. But it is more especially the role of those who by their ordination, their mission or their vows, are more directly and personally consecrated to the good of the whole Church. In our view, this view of obligation, based on the nature of supernatural realities, makes it much stronger than an authoritarian view of obligation which most men today no longer accept.[19]

III. The Liturgy of the Hours in Our Lives

For many of the clergy the 'breviary' was like a foreign en-

19. The cleric or religious bound to the recitation of the Hours does not say Vespers on Maundy Thursday or Good Friday, nor Compline on Holy Saturday, nor the Office of readings at Easter, if he takes part in the evening liturgies of Maundy Thursday, Good Friday and the Easter Vigil.

In art. 97 *The Constitution on the Liturgy* stated, no doubt by analogy to the regulation just referred to: 'Appropriate instances are to be defined by the rubrics in which a liturgical service may be substituted for the divine Office'. The General Instruction does not in fact go into this matter. Without having any special information on the point, we can only suppose it was felt that to try to enumerate all such cases would end up in a mass of rubrical minutiae. This would be to fall back into the unending complications of a juridicism and casuistry. It is for each person to settle his own individual case, in accordance with his conscience and liturgical sense. Moreover, in the life of even the most conscientious priest, the integral recitation of the Hours can be legitimately impeded by a duty of charity or of the apostolate, and not only by a 'sacred action', or properly liturgical action.

clave in their spiritual life, a sort of immoveable rock in the midst of the stream. (While for the great majority of the laity it was something with which they had little or no contact.) This was due to the sheer weight of the Office, to the lack of reforms and adaptations, which still further underlined the absolute nature of the obligation and gave it a place quite apart in the clerical day. People looked elsewhere for nourishment in their spiritual life, and there came a multiplication of devotional exercises: meditations, examinations of conscience, visits to the Blessed Sacrament, retreats . . . These practices, much less strictly obligatory than the recitation of the breviary, hardly existed at all when the Liturgy of the Hours, especially among the monks, was a living reality. The addition of these practices to the recitation of the breviary only made the breviary more burdensome still, as well as emphasizing its apparent sterility.

It seems to us that the renewal of the Liturgy of the Hours, desired by the present reform, will only succeed if this liturgy is harmoniously integrated into the whole spiritual life of the Christian – deliberately, we no longer say 'of the priest'.

The considerable lightening in this liturgy as regards the number of the Hours, and of the psalms within each of the Hours, is not, as we have said, intended to weaken prayer but to improve its quality. This same fact should also make it easier to integrate this liturgy into a person's life of prayer and apostolate.

The Liturgy of the Hours should nourish our *prayer*. The psalms, said calmly and with attention, renew our awareness of God. They accustom us to turning to him, to looking to him, to putting all our hope, all our confidence, the whole of our life in him. The scriptural, patristic and hagiographical readings can only increase our faith and our religious awareness. Certainly they are not in themselves alone sufficient for this, but they can help us by encouraging us to prolong them, to deepen them, and to relate them to modern problems by comparing them with other readings and other reflections. The judicious use of *silence* in the Liturgy of the Hours should not transform it into meditation, but it does prevent us from making this prayer a purely verbal one. It helps us to transform it and to prolong it in deep and personal prayer, and in adoration.

The *lectio divina* is obviously in continuity with the Liturgy of the Hours, since in this liturgy the reading is not approached as if it were an instructive exercise. From the fact that this reading has its place in a liturgy of praise, it is seen as a word of God to which we must respond: it is not just a question of human study, even religious study. It is the first element in a dialogue with God: we listen to God so as to be able to reply to him.

Both *The Constitution on the Liturgy* and the General Instruction on the Liturgy of the Hours indicate that these Hours are valuable as a source of our pastoral life and apostolate.[20] We do not pray merely for ourselves, even if our participation in the liturgy must indeed be 'fruitful', or sanctifying. We pray for those faithful who are specially entrusted to us, for the local church, for the universal Church, and for the whole of humanity of which it is the sacrament. We pray *for* man in the double sense of the word *for*: *for* their intentions, *for* their wellbeing, but also *in* their place, *in* their name.

The fact that we pray to God, that we praise him, that we are at once members and representatives of the Church and of all mankind, already has an apostolic value. Prayer, being the universal duty of every creature, is a reparation for sin and for the fact that God is forgotten. It is thus that the selfless prayer of contemplatives has in itself apostolic value.

The prayer of the Liturgy of the Hours is not only theocentric praise. Through the psalms of supplication, the prayers, the *preces* at Lauds and Vespers, it is also direct intercession for the world.

Our *daily work*, even housework or work in a factory, is linked with the Liturgy of the Hours in a double way. First of all because it is a *cosmic* liturgy, especially by reason of the psalms, which lend a voice of praise to the whole of material creation – 'the earth and all its fullness' – and to the world of nature which work perfects and transforms.

It is a Liturgy of Hours: arranged over the different periods of our day, it gives significance to our *entire* life by throwing its light on all the moments and occupations of our *daily* life. This is particularly evident in the 'Prayers' at Lauds which consecrate the efforts of the day which is about to begin; in the Middle Hour which is above all concerned with sanctifying

20. CL 86; LH 18.

work in the middle of the day; in Compline, which closes the day with an expression of trust.

Finally, and above all, we insisted at the opening of this book on the relationship of the Liturgy of the Hours with the *Mass, the Eucharist*. This is the 'source and summit' of the whole liturgical life and the entire Christian life. It therefore constitutes a special time, having a particular intensity and realism in our day – or at least in our week. But if we say summit, the culminating point, then we imply that there are paths up to the summit and down from it which link it with the plain below. If we say source, we imply that there are streams which carry its life and freshness far and wide. This summit and source should not remain isolated: the different Hours ensure a preparation and continuation throughout the whole of our working day. This prevents the Eucharist from becoming an enclave or island, that we could come to regard as an escape or alibi.

The Liturgy of the Hours thus shares in the cosmic value of the Eucharist, for this is celebrated with bread and wine, 'fruits of the earth and work of human hands'. Under the appearances of bread and wine the Church offers to the Father Christ, first born of every creature, head and recapitulation of the whole cosmos.

The supreme purpose of the Mass is not only to offer Christ to the Father, but to offer ourselves with him – the spiritual sacrifice as the fruit and ultimate purpose of the ritual sacrifice – as it is also the supreme purpose of the Liturgy of the Hours. This latter is the consecration of time, of our time, and that means of ourselves. In its deepest reality the Liturgy of the Hours is thus linked with and liturgically expresses what is the very purpose of the Christian life: the consecration of oneself and of the world to the glory of God for the salvation of men. Or, if you prefer to put it another way: the offering and sacrifice of oneself for the salvation of men, which is at the same time to give glory to God.

The renewal of the Liturgy of the Hours among the Christian people must not be considered as if it were in competition with the Mass and the Sacraments. It should help us to give these their true value by placing them in an atmosphere of praise and of prayer which is both contemplative and apostolic. This should show and guarantee that the whole of the liturgical reform, while making the liturgy more 'human' and better adapted to man's needs, seeks to make it a decisive factor for 'progress in the Christian life'.[21]

21. Article 1 of *The Constitution on the Liturgy* justifies the Council's commitment to liturgical renewal by giving it this objective.